The Perfect Business

MASTER THE 9 SYSTEMS TO GET CONTROL, WORK LESS, AND DOUBLE YOUR PROFIT

John Sheridan

Published by Best Seller Publishing®, Pasadena, CA
Best Seller Publishing® is a registered trademark
Printed in the United States of America.
ISBN: 978-1-946978-39-4

This publication is designed to provide accurate and authoritative information with regard to the subject matter covered. It is sold with the understanding that the publisher is not engaged in rendering legal, accounting, or other professional advice. If legal advice or other expert assistance is required, the services of a competent professional should be sought. The opinions expressed by the authors in this book are not endorsed by Best Seller Publishing® and are the sole responsibility of the author rendering the opinion.

Most Best Seller Publishing® titles are available at special quantity discounts for bulk purchases for sales promotions, premiums, fundraising, and educational use. Special versions or book excerpts can also be created to fit specific needs.

For more information, please write:
Best Seller Publishing®
1346 Walnut Street, #205
Pasadena, CA 91106
or call 1(626) 765 9750
Toll Free: 1(844) 850-3500
Visit us online at: www.BestSellerPublishing.org

*To the owners of small businesses everywhere
who make the sacrifices, take the risks,
and put in the hard work to create value for
everyone who counts on them to succeed.*

Table of Contents

INTRODUCTION:

The Challenge and the Opportunity

Have you ever thought, "I just can't seem to find good people. Nobody wants to work anymore. I'm putting in 80-hour weeks, but no one else around here acts like an owner" or "We keep on getting bigger, but when all is said and done, we're not making any more money than we used to make when we were just three people. The only thing getting bigger is my aggravation"? Or perhaps you've felt that "We have lots of ideas, but we never seem to be able to stick to anything for more than a week. Then it's back to the usual craziness" or "It's always feast or famine; it never gets steady for a long time." If this sounds like you, you're not alone. Dysfunction in small businesses can be seen in the numbers from the U.S. Bureau of Labor Statistics—that 50% of all new businesses don't make it past their fifth birthday.[1]

---

1   Bureau of Labor Statistics (n.d.). *Entrepreneurship and the U.S. Economy.* Retrieved August 10, 2017, from https://www.bls.gov/bdm/entrepreneurship/bdm_chart3.htm

The good news is that it doesn't have to be that way if you are willing to make some changes to yourself and your business.

Consider the following questions, and see if you can answer them now. What are the biggest challenges in your business right now? Are you happy with the results your business yields? How many hours do you work in a week? How do you feel about that? How does your family feel about that? What is the one thing that keeps you up at night? How did you get where you are today? What happens if it stays this way forever? How will it end? Is this what you expected when you got into the business? Put yourself three years into your future. If you and I were talking three years from right now, what must have happened in your business and your life for you to be completely satisfied with the outcome?

Even when you're in a state of overwhelm or if you're stuck in a rut, what you want is pretty clear. You want a machine-like operation that produces consistent, predictable results so you don't have to run around putting out fires caused by stupid mistakes. You want a team that is self-managing so you can have confidence that the business won't fall apart when you go away for a two-week vacation (never had a two-week vacation?). You want steady cash flow and profits that reward you for your hard work and the risks you take every day just being in business. You want *The Perfect Business*, one that provides you with the things you wanted when you began—freedom to do what you want when you want and wealth that builds up over time.

Having been both an operator and an advisor, I've learned that when you look carefully at successful businesses, you realize that they do a lot of different things very well. They might have complex systems, but there are fundamental themes that are common to all of them, and mastering them can transform your business and your life. The challenge is that you're busy, and you think you don't have time to work on the things you know you should be doing, so it can feel overwhelming. It's like standing at the bottom of a mountain before you have to climb it. Fortunately, it's really only your beliefs that stand in the way.

When I set out to create The Perfect Business Framework, I undertook the task of uncovering the fewest possible levers you could pull to get the results you want. This approach is based on the application of the Pareto Principle. Also known as the 80/20 Principle, it's derived from the observation that in any system of inputs and outputs, 80% of the outputs or results are attributable to only 20% of the inputs. Nowhere is this truer than in business. Probably 80% of your profits come from 20% of your customers, 80% of your sales come from 20% of your salespeople, and so on. Along the same lines, it's likely that you produce 80% of your results from 20% of your activity as an owner. I committed myself to discover what those activities were and try to condense them into systems that would be actionable and manageable for someone who is busy running the business day to day. What I created is a framework that will allow you to get the maximum transformation possible by doing only the most important activities. It's designed to provide the "minimum effective dose" of work to make the change you want in your business and your life.

So what is possible for you? Consider the story of Bill, who was a co-owner and CEO of VCI Mobility. VCI Mobility converted vans to become accessible both for the commercial and consumer markets. Bill had been with the company for some years. While it was growing pretty well in terms of sales, it was starting to spiral out of control. Bill would leave his house at 4 or 5 in the morning, be at the office by 6:30, and work into the early evening. Sometimes, he would even stay overnight just to avoid the commute and a sleepless night before heading back to the office, and he was becoming unglued. The morale of the team was going up and down like a roller coaster. They were having some success, but they weren't able to produce quickly enough to keep up, and they were getting farther and farther behind their orders. It was becoming more and more chaotic, and relationships were becoming strained with a lot of "us-versus-them" attitudes infecting the culture.

Bill and his partner believed that they would solve their problems just by increasing sales, but that turned out to be like pouring gasoline onto a fire. As they grew sales, their headaches just multiplied, and because of their lack of control, they didn't have any sense of whether or not they were making any money.

Many of their issues were the direct results of the fact that they didn't have any systems in place. They lost control as the volume and complexity of the work started to overwhelm the team's capacity to produce and Bill's capacity as a leader. It began to take a toll on Bill. He wasn't being much of a father or husband, and he was beginning to feel the physical effects of the stress as well. The way the business was going wasn't sustainable, and he knew something had to change.

We gave Bill our framework of nine systems through which he could stop, think, and understand what was going on in his business, and he began to apply these systems in the business. They brought him back to the basics. He began to get clear on where he was going and why he was going there, and he had to communicate that to his team. We installed systems to measure and monitor lead generation and systems to improve the conversion rate by working on the sales process. We also installed a retention system to keep the customers coming back more often and buying more and other financial control systems and operating measurements. All these started to compound, and we got increasingly greater control, even as the business continued to grow. As we implemented the systems, the team began to experience some victories, which built their confidence. We started winning their hearts and minds. Then we worked on accountability systems, and the team started taking ownership.

Bill went from working almost around the clock to the point where he would be done by 10 o'clock in the morning on most days, simply running meetings and letting his team do the work. The business took on a life of its own. The outcome was that he got what most entrepreneurs dream of—the big check. He had a tremendously successful exit. Then he used the skills and knowledge he had acquired to turn around another business. Today he is on his third turnaround. That's what's possible, and that's why it's worth it.

This book is for the business owner or entrepreneur who has a strong desire to uncover the opportunity that is right in front of their eyes. That could be an opportunity to stop things or start things. It could be to stop the firefighting you're doing or the long hours you're working seven days a week, or it could be to start building up your potential for profit so you can take out more cash to do the things you want to do.

To grab hold of these opportunities, it takes humility to learn and apply proven principles and change the way you do things, and it takes patience to stick with it. The changes don't happen overnight. It's a lot like compound interest or, frankly, like growing your hair—it happens a little bit at a time. But over time, lots of these small changes add up to create dramatic results.

I wrote this book because you asked for it. I spent the early part of my career working for someone else. Although I was extremely fortunate to be a part of some great teams, and I learned a lot from my mentors along the way, I found myself wanting something more. Because it wasn't enough for me to run a business without owning it, I decided to find a business to buy. In my search, I learned two things. One, it's really hard to find a good business to buy. Why? All the businesses for sale were offered by owners who were at the end of their working life, but they had never built the teams or the systems to transform their business into an asset. What they were really selling was a job. If you look for a business to buy, you will find that is there are thousands and thousands of jobs for sale. Two, I learned that I could help these business owners. I felt that because I had made every mistake there was to make in business, I had the experience to see what the owners' challenges were from the outside looking in. When I would talk to them, they would stop me and say, "Wait. Wait. I need to write down what you said. Can you say that again?" Then they would start scribbling away. I thought, "Well, that's interesting. Maybe I can help these people."

I love solving business problems, and I love developing leaders, but what made me want to help them was this: It's important. I'm the son of an entrepreneur and have tremendous respect for someone who gets up every morning to face adversity, works hard, finds a way to satisfy demanding customers, and creates jobs to help drive our economy. You often do this in solitude. You take the risk, and you're often the last to see any benefit. I made it my mission to change this dilemma. I began working with smart, hungry, coachable business owners, and I started to get them remarkable results. As word spread, I found myself being invited to speak to various business groups. After I had given a talk, people would walk up to me and ask me questions. They would ask about my approach to systemizing their small businesses and if I had a book that would help them do it.

My goal in writing this is to share my knowledge and experiences to make a complex undertaking simple to understand and execute so you can get what you want and deserve for taking the risks, trials, and challenges of business ownership.

This book is organized into two parts. Part 1 is about establishing your fundamentals—the big picture—that serve as the foundation for everything else that follows. Part 2 is the step-by-step guide to implementing the most important systems you need to get the results you want.

You might be tempted to jump right ahead into a particular chapter in Part 2 to find a solution to what you think is your most pressing problem, but I encourage you to complete Part 1 first. Why? There are two reasons. First, if you think of your business like a house that you want to improve or expand, it makes no sense to paint over cracks or add walls or other weight to a cracked foundation because it's just going to fall down eventually anyway. You have to go back to the beginning and make sure that the foundation is solid. Sometimes even a little demolition may be required. Second, you need to know the difference between what to do and how to do it. In other words, if I give you a saw or a hammer, it doesn't necessarily mean that you know how, when, and where to use it. Once you understand that, though, you can use those skills to improvise, adapt, and design in a safe and effective way. You need to know what to do and why you need to do it before you get into how you are going to do it.

So begin by reading Part 1 and making sure you have a solid foundation before you embark on Part 2 and the specifics for how to create your perfect business.

PART 1

The Big Picture

CHAPTER 1

What Drives
Predictable Profits

Growing your business can seem like a fight. In fact, crisis management can become your specialty if you work at it hard enough. Working harder has its limits, though, both physically and mentally. Not knowing what will come next and dealing with the unexpected all the time can take its toll. Then there are the financial sacrifices. You understand you have to reinvest, but when will that end? Despite all the challenges, failure is not an option. No entrepreneur I know is willing to give up and get a job. Every once in a while, though, you see what does work in somebody else's business—the business of a customer or a friend or supplier. You can see that they only work four days a week, they have a lot of nice things or a second home, and their business seems to be like a well-oiled machine. When you see it, you say to yourself, "Why not me? I want what they have."

THREE KEY DRIVERS OF VALUE

I do a lot of work searching for businesses to buy on behalf of my clients and myself. I get to see two or three businesses a week, and I'm forced to look deeply into each one very quickly to try to understand its value. While the value of a business may seem to be driven by how much cash it produces—its profitability—that is only part of it. It's also important to understand how predictable those profits are. The predictability of the profits comes from three areas, and these are the key drivers of value. The three areas are the *model*, the quality of the *people*, and the quality of the *systems*.

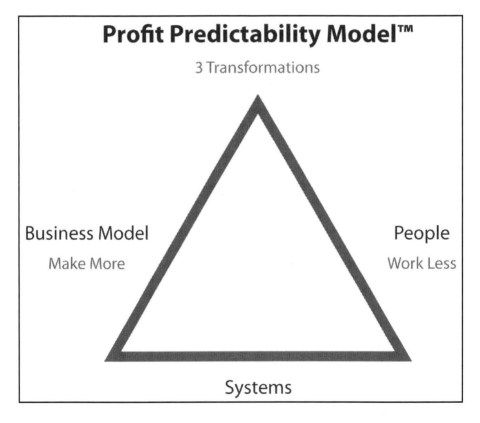

Figure 1-1, Profit Predictability Model

The model. The model is what your business offers to the marketplace and how compelling that offer is. In other words, it is the value proposition: the way you create value for your customer. Is that value proposition unique? Do you stand out from everyone else who is trying to do the same thing? Also, is it compelling enough to make the customer want to part with their cash to experience that value? Another component of the model is the nature of your customer concentration and vendor concentration. Do only a few of your customers provide a lot of your revenue? Are you particularly dependent on one vendor? Also, what is the nature of your revenue stream? Is it project based or more recurring? How far into the future can you reliably predict your cash flow and sales? Is the offering more of a vitamin or an aspirin for your customers?

The value you create can be measured roughly by the rate of gross profit you generate. In other words, if you are making a 30% gross profit, what is more important than that number in itself is how it compares to your competitors. Is that high or low relative to your competitors? Typically, these elements of the model are not changeable quickly. If you have been in business for a while, and you're selling successfully, there is not a lot you can do to change that overnight. Likewise, changing your customer concentration or shifting from a project-based business to a recurring revenue model based business takes a lot of time and effort.

The people. The second driver of people is all about the strength of the management team and the culture and how this has changed over time. As the business grows, the skill sets that worked yesterday won't necessarily work today. And some businesses develop faster than the people running them. If there are issues in this area, it's going to take some time to work through and improve them to the point where you create a stronger business.

The systems. It all rests on the third leg—the systems. Does your business run on you, or does it run on systems? How dependent is it on you as the owner? If we were to take you out of it and send you away for a month, what would happen? Would your business continue to grow and thrive or at least survive, or would it start to fall apart? How you feel while you're on vacation (if you've ever taken one) is probably a good, quick estimate of how strong your systems are.

Your success or lack thereof can be traced back to these three drivers. Any challenge in the areas of time, money, and people can be traced back to one of these three. When problems occur, most owners mistakenly look at fixing the people before they look at fixing the systems. They tend to believe that "If I just had better people, things would be a lot different." That is typically not the case, however. And again, there is not much you can do to change the model rapidly. The opportunities usually lie in the systems. Developing the systems to the point where they run the business instead of you is the fastest path to predictable profits.

The key drivers of our Profit Predictability Model can be developed and strengthened over time. The quest of systemizing your business so that it generates predictable profits is a journey that will unfold step by step. Here's what it will look like.

Five Levels of Business Maturity

Every business goes through a progression of five stages. The first stage is what we will call *survival*. It is the roller coaster that most owners are on when they are in an immature business, which is characterized by the battle cry of "Sell, sell, sell!" followed by, "Make, make, make!" It's the feast-or-famine cycle where it's first about finding the work and then it's about doing the work. There is no consistency in the flow of leads or sales, so it's very stressful and chaotic. Many businesses manage to survive this stage, and some even manage to survive many years, but very few break through it and get to the next stage that we will call *acceptance*. This level is achieved when the customers are willing to pay for what the business offers on a consistent basis. In this stage, the business may still rely on the owner working long and hard hours every day. The critical shift comes when the business has reached the stage of *systemization*. It no longer relies solely on the hard work of the owner because the systems are developed to the point where they can start to take over and create value. This is the shift that most small businesses will never make. Once the systems are developed to a certain point, the next stage of maturity is characterized by the development of its *people*. They need to be educated, trained, coached, and developed so they can operate the systems at a higher level.

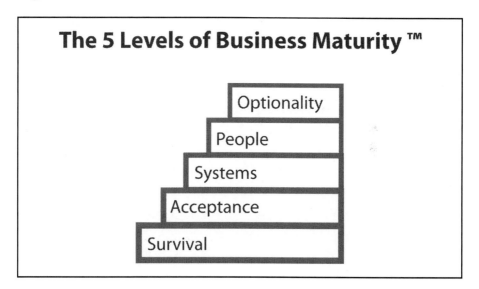

Figure 1-2, The 5 Levels of Business Maturity.

If a business matures through these stages successfully, the result is the creation of an asset; something of value. That is where you reach what is called *optionality*, which means you have choices about what comes next. You can sell the business, scale it, or lifestyle it. You can sell the business and go on to do whatever you want to do next. You can scale it, which is mainly taking what you have done and repeating it over and over again to multiply the results. A franchise is a good example of that approach. Or you can "lifestyle" it. If you had a business that only required you to work two days a week, and it yielded a predictable profit, why would you want to sell that? You could just keep it and enjoy your time for other things aside from business. Those are the stages your business will go through, but what about you as a leader?

THE OWNER'S JOURNEY

If your business is to move up the five stages of maturity, you will have to change as well. Your role is going to change along the way. You probably started off as someone who is doing it all; that is, being the technician, doing the selling, doing the making, and scrambling to manage the day-to-day work. At a certain point, you hired people, or maybe you already had some people, and you learned that you had to become a "MOP," which stands for manager of people, so you have to learn new skills. This means you can grow the business a little bit more. As the number of people increases, however, the natural limit of what you can do to manage all of them hits you in the face, and you have to learn a new set of skills—to become a "MOM," a manager of managers, and empower other people to step up and help do part of your management job. If you adapt to that role successfully, you can move on from there. Eventually, you will reach a point where you have to learn yet another set of skills, and that is to become an "LOM," or leader of managers. You will no longer manage day to day, but instead focus solely on leading and developing other managers.

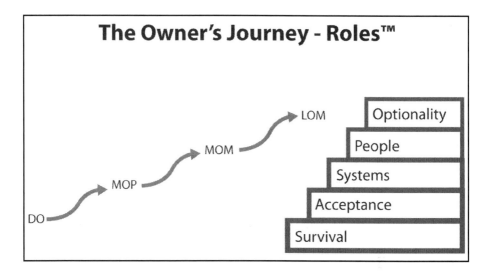

Figure 1-3, The Owner's Journey – Roles.

When you start out, you are focused on critical skills like selling, firefighting, or managing to have just enough cash in the bank, and you're largely in a reactive state, which is appropriate when the business is immature. It doesn't necessarily have anything to do with the age of the business. There are businesses that are quite advanced in years that have never gotten beyond a reactive state. As the business grows, its size, complexity, and velocity will increase, and the number of relationships between people will grow exponentially. Then the skills that used to be important will become less and less critical on a day-to-day basis for you as the owner. You will have to learn how to let go of those things. Conversely, the skills of planning, delegating, and strategizing are not too relevant in the beginning stages when you're worried about making payroll or getting the next order to keep the doors open. But those skills will become more important as the business grows in size, velocity, complexity, and the number of relationships, and then you have to acquire those.

THREE SHIFTS YOU HAVE TO MAKE AS THE OWNER

There are three shifts that you have to make as an owner. As you can see, there is learning that has to happen. That is the first major shift. The second major shift is that you have to let go of the day-to-day crisis management, firefighting, and even selling if you are to transform into the manager and leader you need to be to grow the business beyond those barriers we talked about earlier in the five stages. The third major shift is that you have to stop doing stupid things—repeating mistakes because you reinvent the wheel over and over again.

As an example of learning, take Tom, who is a successful manager of a reconditioning and manufacturing operation that serves the industrial market. He began the business as a road warrior, a sales representative, going out, cracking accounts, and getting jobs, which is what he truly loves to do. He managed to acquire employees, space, machinery and equipment, and customers, and he built up a successful operation over 10 years. He found, however, that the skills he used on the road didn't translate to inside the four walls of the building, and he had to learn some new skills. He had to learn how to acquire sales people, which meant that being a sales representative wouldn't cut it anymore. He had to learn how to manage people. He had to learn how to become a sales manager, and he had to learn how to become a president. It became an ongoing evolution and transformation for him.

Then consider the story of Bob, who ran a drilling business. As he grew, he learned that what he loved to call a "family business" had to evolve to a more professional organization, and that meant introducing an organizational hierarchy to clarify the roles and responsibilities for his growing team. This was difficult for him to accept because he felt bad about the idea of one person being perceived as above another person, and it took him several years to change his thinking. So what took Tom some months to learn to do took Bob years. Everyone learns at a different rate, but if you want to or if you're forced to—when your survival depends on it— you can and will do it.

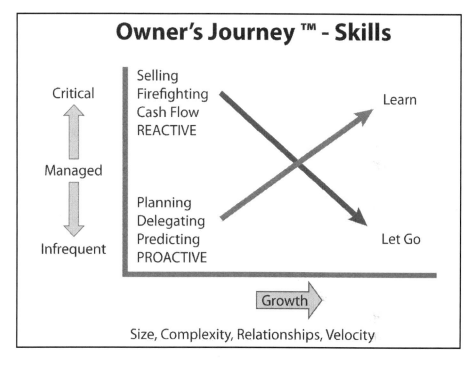

Figure 1-4, The Owner's Journey – Skills.

When it comes to the shift of letting go, you can think of Jim, who like many business owners I've encountered, was unable to let go of certain things until he had to. For example, he had 20 people in his business, but he was still the one processing the payroll. Or consider Mike, who was struggling with running his business but refused to get help in the form of a personal assistant. He understood perfectly that he was wasting a lot of his time, but his inability to let go emotionally was holding him back. It wasn't until Jim and Mike made those changes that they realized how mistaken they had been for not having done it sooner. As the owner, you are the king. You have a lot of power, and you get to set the rules. If you expect your employees to take ownership of their jobs but are unwilling to let go and are not approachable or open, it's very difficult for them when you get angry because they made a mistake or they made a decision without consulting you. It's hard to see because they won't be candid enough with you to tell you that what you're doing is not smart. They won't let you know when they are essentially being punished for trying to take ownership. The emotional challenge of letting go is the second shift you have to make.

Tom can also serve as an example when it comes to the third shift: Stop doing stupid things. Tom's business requires his team to work with very detailed engineering drawings, and there are constantly new revisions and variations of these drawings. After 15 years in business, the drawings had never been systemized or organized and were kept in four different offices in his shop. The business grew to the point where it would take two hours to find the right drawing to complete a job—a task that would take about five minutes when the documents were organized. It wasn't until someone on the outside said, "Hey, wait a minute, this is really stupid," that Tom had a blinding flash of the obvious and realized how much time he lost simply because of his disorganization. If you do proposals in your business, think about Mike and his business. It used to take Mike four or five hours to create a proposal to quote a customer. After we systemized it, it only took him 25 minutes. In the course of a jam-packed week, that is a huge gain. What is the antidote to doing stupid things over and over? It's systems. Systems will set you free. It's the fastest path to predictable profits. Learning and letting go underlie everything that follows, but it's the systems that will take you there.

CHAPTER 2

The Perfect Business Framework

What do I see when I walk into a poorly performing business? I see the symptoms of life without systems: people running around putting out fires, lots of mistakes, waste, unpredictable costs, unpredictable cash flow, and weak margins. I see annoyed customers leaving for the competition because of mistakes, delays, incomplete orders, or a variety of unmet expectations or because they just don't feel loved. I see employees who are making bad decisions or bad judgments and are punished for their mistakes by managers who don't know how to manage. Since the employees can't win, they become frustrated and leave, and that causes a lot of turnover. Or what is worse, they check out mentally, but don't leave; they stay and become a drag on the organization. I see an owner who is aggravated and asking, "What am I doing wrong?" They can't sleep at night because they know that if one of these mistakes happens a certain way, it will cost them their best customer or if it's a life safety issue, it may even cause an accident, and then it's game over for the business.

When I walk into a business that is running like a well-oiled machine, I see a different set of symptoms and experience a very different feeling. The mistakes and surprises all around the various processes in the business are fewer. Quality is predictable and controlled, costs are lower, and profits are higher and more predictable. The customers' experience matches the brand promise, so they are happy, and they stay and refer more business. The employees aren't making it up as they go; they are accountable to a performance standard, and they transform to that standard, or they are no longer on the team. I experience an overall consistent experience for both the customers and the team with accountability built into it. The energy is better.

As a consumer, you too have experienced a well-run business. Just think about Starbucks, for example. In 2016, Starbucks had more than 25,000 stores, more than 300,000 employees, and over $21 billion in revenue. How do they create a consistent experience around a customized, handcrafted drink? They draw from the same talent pool you do and pay close to market wages, so they have no particular advantage as far as labor goes. Nevertheless, they manage to get their 300,000 employees in 25,000 locations to deliver consistency of experience. Their systems are what allow them to do this. Without the systems, they wouldn't be able to control any aspect of their customers' experience. Operating each location with the same systems every day enables them to deliver the consistency of experience. As long as they do that, they deliver the experience you have come to expect.

If you're not excited about systemizing your business right now, you probably have some resistance to overcome. To overcome the inertia, consider the leverage that systems offer—how they allow you to get more work done with less effort. If you needed to change a tire on your car, it would be silly to get five or six friends to lift up the bumper instead of simply taking advantage of using a jack, turning the crank and lifting the car up almost effortlessly. The same applies to systems in businesses. They ensure quality and speed, keep the cost controlled, and most importantly, create consistency in your customers' experience—both your external customers as well as your team—your internal customers.

Systems are the antidote to the poison of complexity. Complexity creeps into any enterprise as it grows and its magnitude increases because people like it. They like to solve problems. But as the details mount, the limits of their memory start to become clear, and the complexity starts to become the enemy of profit. Systematization forces simplification because it causes you to ask questions like, "Why do we do things this way?" Just sitting down with the team, looking at how you do things, and asking, "Why?" surfaces all the complexity that doesn't need to be in the system.

Systems create value because they institutionalize the way you serve the customer. Because they are independent of any one individual's judgment, they prevent anyone from becoming a single point of failure. The operators of the systems, your team, might change over time, but if robust systems are doing the work, you won't be held hostage to someone who has all the important operating knowledge in their head.

You might object to systematization because you think your business is somehow unique and can't be systemized, but that is false. The truth is that in any business, no matter what you do, at least 80% of the work is routine. Even if you create customized projects for each customer, 80% of the process you go through is the same time after time and can therefore be systemized. If it's routine, it's ideally suited to be systemized, and you can get the benefits of consistency. Now, if 80% can be systemized, that is a lot, and you're standing on the wrong side of a lot of work. That is where The Perfect Business Framework can help break down the big challenge of systemization into the few most essential steps.

THE PERFECT BUSINESS FRAMEWORK

How do we understand the challenges of systemizing your business so we can develop a strategy to overcome them and build an asset in the simplest, most effective way?

First, we have to understand the goal—what do we want from the perfect business? If you're like most owners, the answers to that question fall into one of three categories of desired outcomes. First and foremost is *freedom*. Ownership should bring you the benefit of independence in terms of control over your destiny and the freedom to choose what you want to do with your time. Of course, it doesn't always work out that way for most business owners, who end up becoming a servant of their business instead of its master. This is, however, the outcome most often cited when business owners are asked why they chose the path of entrepreneurship. The second desired outcome is *cash flow,* and that can be expressed in terms of being able to set your personal income at a level that provides the lifestyle you choose. It can also be expressed by your expectation of receiving a large sum of cash when you eventually exit your business. The third desired outcome of the perfect business is *growth,* and by that we mean satisfaction not just in terms of wealth and achievement, but the fulfillment that results from engagement with your team, helping others, and developing as a person.

To achieve these outcomes requires building and balancing systems in three areas of your business—*team, customers,* and *direction and control.* The systems you build for your team will be designed to create accountability above all. That's what is needed to get a group of people to act as if they themselves were owners.

The systems you build for your customer are planned for creating velocity—a steady source of the right customers to keep the cash flow healthy. These are the systems designed to find (and keep!) the right customers. The third area, direction and control, are your systems that execute the day-to-day management.

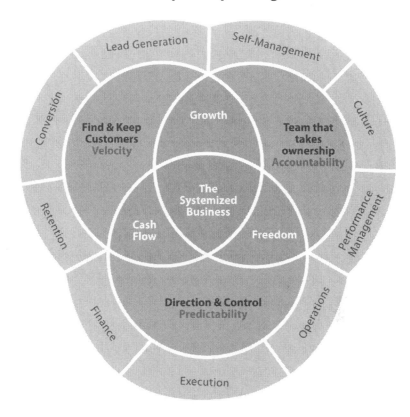

Figure 2-1, The Perfect Business Framework.

Without strength in all three areas, bad things will happen. Without accountability in your team, you will have no peace. If there's no velocity to find and keep customers, you will have no cash flow. And without predictability, you will have no control. There are systems to build in all three areas; the framework identifies the most essential ones. Each area has three basic systems to master.

Team. In the area of team, first comes the system of *self-management*, which is how you allocate your time, manage your mindset, and control your focus on the few things that make a difference in the growth of your business over a range of timeframes—from the long term all the way down to the precious minutes of each working hour. Next is the system of *culture*—how you define it, teach it, reinforce it, and recognize it so that team members think and act like you would even when you're not there with them. Third is the system of *performance management*, which encompasses everything about your team members' experience with you and the organization:

- The hiring process, which includes recruiting, screening, selection, onboarding, training, and developing new players.
- The management process, which is the day-to-day management techniques, performance feedback and evaluation, and compensation and incentive models.
- An accountability plan, which includes performance standards and measurements, all of which serve to align and engage the team to ensure that everyone is working together for the common goal.

Direction and control. In direction and control, first comes the system of *finance*, which is the reporting, cash flow control, capital budgeting, cost accounting, and operating measures you need to make evidence-based decisions instead of seat-of-the-pants guesses. Second is the system of *execution*—the day-to-day communication and control techniques that track and ensure that everyone does what they say they will do. Third is the *operations* system, which is the set of repeatable processes for how you create value in the production of your service or product. It's where you control the cost, quality, and throughput for the benefit of the customer.

Customer. In the customer area, the first element is the system of *lead generation*. That is the process for how you find and acquire new customers in a profitable way, which can only be done if you can measure the effectiveness of your strategies and engineer a budget-driven machine that produces the right number of qualified leads to meet your sales goals. Once you have the leads, you need a system of *conversion*, which is the process by which you turn your qualified leads into paying customers systematically so you are not dependent on any one salesperson's personality to win business. Finally, you must have a system of *customer retention* because the most efficient way to grow sales is to begin by first, stop losing customers. If you don't have a system for that, adding customers is like pouring water into a bucket with a hole in it. Your customer retention depends on what you do to keep them. That includes your communication strategy, standards of service, and other systems to recognize what they want and give it to them.

This set of nine systems from the three areas are the building blocks that deliver velocity, accountability, and predictability—the key ingredients of a business that is truly built to be an asset.

IMPLEMENTATION: THE 4-STEP SYSTEM BUILDING PROCESS

As you go about implementing each of these systems, you will find that there is a process for implementing the changes you need to make. That is the 4-Step System Building Process, which consists of *prioritizing, analyzing, optimizing,* and *institutionalizing*.

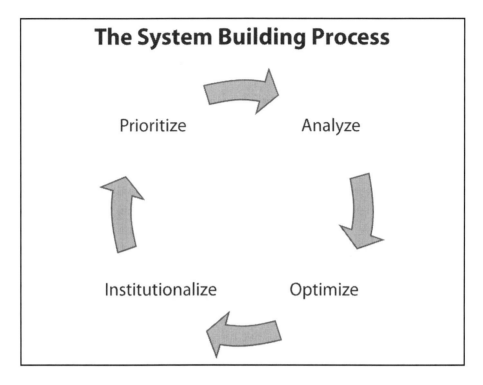

Figure 2-2, The System Building Process.

Prioritize. You want to use the framework to identify the opportunities and decide which ones to work on first according to which ones make the highest impact with the least amount of effort.

Analyze. Before you make any changes to a particular system, you need to analyze it. Understand exactly how the work is currently done by including all the players involved and writing it down. Then see if you can baseline some measurement of the throughput so you can measure improvement.

Optimize. Documenting will in itself show opportunities for improvement. There is no need to reinvent any wheels, though. It's best to use proven processes and adapt them to your particular set of circumstances. Later you will see plenty of examples of systems you can install in each of the nine areas.

Institutionalize. The final task is to institutionalize—to make it stick so it becomes permanent. This means managing change, which is mostly changing habits. Most habits, depending on how deeply entrenched they are, might take about 60 days to change. The first couple of months, you need to put energy into and focus on teaching and reinforcing whatever changes have to occur, and then you must set up key performance indicators or reports or cross checks to make sure that they happen.

REPEAT THE PROCESS

When you have done all of the four steps, you repeat the process of prioritizing, analyzing, optimizing, and institutionalizing again and again until you have built each of the nine systems to the point where they support the business to the level you desire. That is how you break down the challenge into manageable, bite-size chunks. With focus and persistence, the wins will start to accumulate, giving you and your team more confidence to tackle more and more. There will be resistance along the way, but success builds momentum, and that momentum might overcome the rock-throwers who might stand in your way.

As you undertake this endeavor, it is important to understand what is going to happen before it happens so you can be well positioned to make it as successful as possible. That means understanding what change will bring out in your team and how to deal with it, and how to arrange all the factors you can to maximize your chance for success. That is what we will look at next.

CHAPTER 3

Overcoming the Challenge of Implementation

There will be bumps along the road to building your systemized business. Building new systems or fixing old ones means learning new skills, developing new habits, finding new approaches, and fixing new problems. All that can be summed up as change. Change brings with it obstacles that you need to overcome or at least manage if you are going to succeed. When you have tried to bring about a change in your business in the past, you have probably experienced one of several things. You might have found your team to be great at talking about and deciding to solve problems but lacking in the follow-through to make things actually change. Or you might have found yourself making a mistake and determining what the cause of it was and finding a way to fix it but never quite getting around to the fix. Then, when you make the same mistake again, you get frustrated. Or you probably have found that some on your team can't handle change. They either resist passively or may even resist actively and throw rocks at anything to do with change. As a result, you are understandably leery about repeating that cycle. You are concerned that the team might think, "Well, it's just another fad. We've done this before, and they'll give up after a few days."

It's worth understanding how to stack the deck in your favor to bring about what you want. What you want is to make the new way of doing things automatic—no more reinventing things that have been done many times before. You want to start out with a momentum that builds on itself, which sustains the change well into the future. You want everyone to work together as a team instead of at cross-purposes, with everyone in line toward the goal. That way, change, whether it's changing a system or strategy or implementing a new way of doing things, becomes something that has its own process, a specific approach that overpowers all the inertia and resistance so the new way happens the way you want.

HillCon, a 40-year-old residential construction company, serves a niche that focuses on large, complex, long-term projects. In this world, change orders are a big part of managing the business. These change orders can go wrong for several reasons. Sometimes, as a project is moving forward, the clients can't make decisions, or they don't make decisions on time. The changes often happen simultaneously, so it's easy to lose control of a project. The changes are also dynamic, and many of them are interconnected and driven by complex variables. Add to this that the communication modes for them are mixed. The communication could happen verbally or in writing, via email, via text messages, or via plans with revisions upon revisions. When the paperwork can't keep up with the construction pace, it's a recipe for disaster. There comes a time when all the change orders finally hit. They snowball into one gigantic mess and become a big surprise. It's a lot like taking a large party to a restaurant, and then when you get the check, you look at it and say to yourself, "Who ordered all this food?!" You can't believe how big it is. It results in a lot of ill will and a loss of trust. Nasty negotiations ensue, and everyone loses something. Even with 40 years of experience and a good reputation, HillCon experienced these problems repeatedly. They had tried to fix them before, but as they grew without written systems, all the training, to the extent that it existed at all, was informal and done by "word of mouth." When they brought new project managers into the business, their practices would mutate a little bit. Every once in a while, things went terribly wrong, and they experienced a lot of pain. On one project, it got so bad that the change orders snowballed into hundreds of thousands of dollars near the end of the project, which is usually when everyone's emotions are running high. They submitted their bill and held their breath. Then they heard the dreaded words: "I'm not paying for this!" They knew they needed a new approach and had to make a lasting change.

RESISTANCE TO CHANGE

Change brings resistance, and that resistance has to be overcome for success to happen, so it is important to understand the roots of the resistance. Usually, it comes from some fear. It could be a fear of losing money, a fear of embarrassment, a fear of losing face, a fear of losing a relationship, a fear of losing trust, or a fear of losing a sense of comfort or predictability. Resistance can also come from sheer sloth or lack of knowledge. Or it can be a result of limiting beliefs or deeply entrenched habits. Wherever it comes from, you or anyone on your team can bring it into the organization, and it can appear without anyone being conscious of it.

When we analyzed the roots of resistance at HillCon, we discovered that the project managers were faced with several challenges. One was conflict. The project managers didn't want to risk getting into arguments or confrontations with clients because their performance was measured in part by the quality of the clients' experience. So it was easier for them to avoid resolving important issues under the false belief that it would help maintain their relationships. The burden of documentation and communication in following up was another point of resistance—it slowed them down, so they would skimp on thorough communications in the interest of speeding through their day to keep their projects on schedule. Competing incentives were a third. The desire to drive the construction project forward competed against slowing down the project to take care of the paperwork, the back and forth of the communication, and involving all the players in the changes. They had to overcome all of this resistance. Resistance to change can be powerful—so powerful that the only thing that causes it to be overcome is a crisis, and that was what happened at HillCon. They were up against the wall. The magnitude of the situation was an existential threat to their business.

THE 3 FORCES FOR CHANGE

You want to take advantage of every possible way you can help your team and yourself overcome the powerful force of resistance when faced with making a change in the way you do things. To do that, you need to leverage three forces: *commitment, competence,* and *context*. These are the three forces that help you to overcome the powers of resistance. To leverage the power of commitment, you want to maximize the depth and strength of your desire to undertake the task ahead. In the area of competence, you need to learn (or borrow or buy) new skills when you need to do things differently. In the area of context, you want to arrange the structure or environment to make the change as easy and long lasting as possible. The goal in any implementation, whether it be implementing a new system or anything else, is to combine the power of these three forces to crush the resistance that will inevitably stand in the way of your goals.

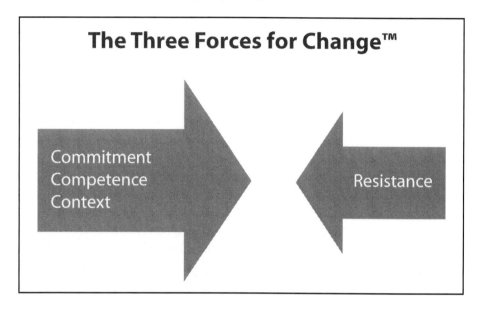

The Three Forces for Change™

Commitment
Competence
Context

Resistance

Figure 3-1, The 3 Forces for Change

Here are some specific ways you can build power in each of the three forces.

Commitment. Start with a strong vision, a vividly clear picture of what success looks like on which everyone can agree. You also need to understand your *why*—the reason you are undertaking this task—and build an emotional connection to that reason. Be candid with yourself. Ask the question, "Is this a good idea, a great thought, or a *must*?" If it's not a "must," that's not enough. You can also leverage the magical power of peer pressure. It works by tapping into our deep, fundamental desire to be seen as reliable and accepted by our peers. So make a public commitment. Bring up the statement you want your company to live up to in front of your peers. HillCon's *why* was the fact that their jobs were on the line; that the company itself was at risk. To build their vision, we found a success story from a similar company that had experienced the same problem and solved it, and then we modeled the vision after their success. It required a new commitment to a system that was already developed, but that wasn't being followed. When we completed planning the change, we gathered all the stakeholders and asked each one of them individually to make a public commitment to make the change happen.

Competence. Leveraging the force of competence involves learning new skills and developing new habits to make the change happen. At HillCon, we provided the project managers with exact scripting to handle the conversations with the clients and then drilled them on it. We taught them new documentation techniques that were fast and easy, and we taught them how to use email templates to expedite the communication.

In any situation, there is something good happening, and the challenge is to find and use it to your advantage. At HillCon, we found one project manager who was a star at managing change orders with clients. We dug into what he was doing, captured it, and then we leveraged his knowledge and asked him to teach the remaining project managers the techniques to improve their skills.

It's likely that your team will have to build new habits. Habits are a key driver of our behaviors minute to minute— it has been estimated that they account for 40% of what we do. So we can take advantage of that power wherever discipline is needed. It generally takes about 60 days of disciplined effort to form a new habit, but once it's formed, it takes on great momentum. One thing you can do to create new habits is to set up a trigger, a specific event that will trigger a desired behavior. At HillCon, the practice was that when a client site meeting would end, all the parties would scatter in different directions and go about their day. Now a site meeting doesn't end until the project manager has written down and completed the summary notes, so even though the client may leave, the project manager doesn't end the meeting officially until he has completed documentation and communication to "trap" the decisions and open issues.

Context. As willpower is only so strong, you can't rely on commitment and competence alone; you need support, and that comes from the environment or the context, which means removing any obstacles that are in the processes to make it easy. It begins with reporting—creating visibility into the predictors and results that are reviewed and acted upon at regular intervals. For HillCon, we created an open change order report that was reviewed weekly and that generated follow-up actions to close out any open change orders. Another tactic you can employ is to remove choice by forcing an approval or making it easy with a software process.

Here's an example. I have a problem with cookies. If there are cookies on the counter after dinner, I'll reach for them and eat them, maybe even all of them, probably all at once. I have discovered, though, that if there are no cookies to reach for, I don't eat them. Of course, I can't because I have no choice. They aren't there to eat. We applied that tactic to HillCon by making a structural change of taking away the project managers' authority to buy any new materials unless and until there was an authorized change order from the client. As a result, the project could not move forward if a change order that required some material was not yet resolved. We gave them no choice.

You can also remove any friction in the process by streamlining anything that has to be done by making it easier, faster, and not overly complex. In addition, you need to align your incentives or punishments, whether they are monetary or not, to the actions you want to see. At HillCon, we did this by posting the results publicly on the open change order report and relying on the natural, effective peer pressure to bring about compliance. When you encounter rock-throwers (and it seems there is always a rock-thrower on a team), there are two strategies you can employ. One is to enlist them by acknowledging their existence and persuading them to join in the effort. The other is simply to remove them from the collection of stakeholders and get them out of the way. Finally, you can divide the task into smaller steps to get more wins faster, thus creating momentum, and that gives you a head start.

These tactics for implementing a new system go deeper than basic project planning; they go to the psychological attributes that we all have that either support change or allow resistance to win the day. HillCon, I'm happy to say, had a happy ending. Although their record isn't perfect, they haven't had any more close calls or tactical surprises during large projects since they implemented the new system. In fact, since change orders are now estimated and reported in a more timely fashion, their financial reporting has greatly improved.

QUESTIONS TO EASE YOUR TRANSITION

To make your transition to a systemized business much easier, when you are at the planning stage, stop and think through the following questions before you move ahead:

1. What does success look like, specifically?
2. Why is it important to get this right? What happens if you don't get it right? What is the emotional reason to which you can connect?
3. What are the critical steps that you have to choreograph to take away choice? Where could you step up triggers to program the behaviors you want?
4. Who is the star on the team who already masters this particular skill? How can you get this person to teach the rest of the team?

5. What is the first small win you can build into the implementation plan?
6. What new skills do you have to learn to make this work? Who will teach those skills?
7. What or who are the obstacles standing in the way?
8. How can you make it too easy?
9. What incentives and punishments can you implement to encourage the desired behaviors?
10. What tool can you use to bring about a public commitment and peer pressure to ensure compliance? Is it a report, a chart, or some automated alert?

All the effort is worthwhile, so let's revisit one more reason to begin this journey.

CHAPTER 4

Doubling Your Profit Using The 9 Systems

As a natural outcome of the drive to survive, most entrepreneurs and business owners focus on getting bigger. They believe that one more sale will make the difference. This belief is ingrained in everything they do and becomes a driving force in their behavior, which causes them to focus on the top line and do whatever they can think of to grow sales. They end up trying a new advertising idea or hiring a new salesperson and hoping they are the silver bullet. Digging deeper requires discipline, diligence, and patience, and it's not a lot of fun for most entrepreneurs. Eventually, sometimes too late, they realize that "Hey, my company was making more money when it was half the size, and it gave me half the headaches as well."

There is a better way, and that is a systematic approach to growth that starts with understanding the information that is already in the business and using it in a systematic way to grow it. It's about implementing small, manageable projects that make improvements in the specific drivers that determine growth, which results in reliance on systems instead of a particular person or the latest marketing fad. Because it's repeatable, it can be sustainable. This approach allows you not only to double your profit but also grow it exponentially over time.

Before undertaking this project, keep in mind that bigger is not better. It's like the old saying, "It's not what you make; it's what you keep." Translated into your business, it's not how big your sales might be that matters; what matters is what your profit is and how much cash you can take out of it. Growing your top line is of no use if you can't grow your profit. There is no sense in adding customers and the burdens that come with them on to the team and the systems if there is no incremental profit to justify it. That is often what happens, however, when the focus is on the top line. Everyone on the team drives more sales when they instead should be driving toward better ones. This is a mental shift that the owner has to undertake before the rest of the team can learn it.

Also, to quote Warren Buffett, "It is not necessary to do extraordinary things to get extraordinary results." You can achieve much improvement by executing a series of small changes that produce an overall benefit that is much greater than the sum of the parts when they are combined. This systematic approach makes it easier to break up the challenge into small pieces that can be implemented one at a time and built into day-to-day operations so that they stay in place.

THE FIVE LEVERS OF PROFIT GROWTH

Do you really understand exactly how your business makes money? The financial model of your business can be analyzed through the lens of the five levers of profit growth. The five levers are the underlying variables or inputs that you can manipulate that determine the outcomes in your financial model. Breaking down the financial model of your business into these levers is where you begin. By digging deeper and understanding these drivers, you deconstruct how you make money. Then you can see clearly the impact you can make by focusing on these points of leverage and influence them. By improving each one, you can create an outcome that is much greater than the sum of the parts. Now let's look at these five levers of growth.

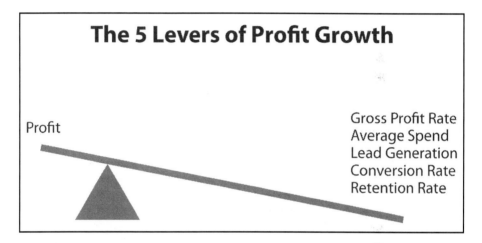

The 5 Levers of Profit Growth

Profit

Gross Profit Rate
Average Spend
Lead Generation
Conversion Rate
Retention Rate

Figure 4-1, The Five Levers of Profit Growth

Gross profit. The first lever is gross profit, which is the profit generated by sales after subtracting the cost of goods sold but before taking out overhead expenses, such as rent, utilities, salaries, and others. It is an expression of how much value you are creating for your customer. The more value you create, the better your gross profit rate is.

Average spend. The second lever is average spend by each customer. You obtain your average spend figure by dividing your sales by the number of customers you served over a year. Some customers will buy only once and never come back, while others might buy many times per year. Likewise, some customers will buy only a small amount, while others will make big purchases. The overall average is composed of how much they buy and how often they buy from you.

Lead generation. The third lever is lead generation. Leads are your prospective customers—anyone who has responded to your marketing, be it through your website, display advertising, outbound sales efforts, or whatever the case might be, and said they are interested in more information.

Conversion rate. Not all leads become customers, and that is where the fourth lever, conversion rate, comes into play. Conversion rate refers to the proportion of the leads that convert into new customers as a result of your sales process. You can think of conversion rate as the measure of the effectiveness of your sales efforts.

Customer retention rate. The fifth lever is customer retention rate. Not all your customers stay with you for life; some die or move away, but most customers will actually leave because they think you don't care about them. There is no point in welcoming new customers and going to all the effort of marketing and selling to them if other customers are leaving you. It's like pouring water into a leaking bucket. That is why customer retention is a lever you can use to grow profit.

APPLYING THE LEVERS

Let's look at how a business can increase its profit by influencing the five levers. As an example, we'll look at Suburban Management, a company in the business of providing building maintenance services to commercial and residential property owners. They had $1.8 million in revenue at a gross profit rate of 40%, which yielded a gross profit of $720,000. It cost Suburban $50,000 a month to be in business, to keep the lights on and pay the rent, and that general and administrative expense translated to $600,000 per year. By subtracting that from the $720,000 gross profit, we found that they had a profit of 120,000, which was roughly 7% of revenue.

The owner of Suburban Management wanted to grow the company's profit over three years to increase its value so he could sell it when he retired. To help him build a plan for him to grow the business, we analyzed the five levers in it so we could decide how to use them to push up the profit so he could realize greater value upon his exit.

To determine the five levers, we need to expand this idea of sales into its constituent parts. Let's begin with the top line of $1.8 million and figure out where it came from. The company had 450 customers who each year spent an average amount composed of how often they bought and the amount they bought for each time. After analyzing their sales and customers, they found that the average customer spent $4,000 over the course of a year. Some bought a few times, and some bought a lot, but on average, each client spent $4,000 in a year. The revenue, the top line, was $4,000 per client multiplied by 450 clients—$1.8 million. To understand where the customers came from, we have to break down that number as well. There were two sets of customers: a set of repeat customers—the net number of customers who they had served the year before after those lost through attrition—and a set of new customers who they had added as a result of their marketing and sales efforts. Suburban had 400 repeat customers and 50 new customers; 450 in total.

Let's break this down even a bit further to get to the five levers. We'll start with the repeat customers. Suburban's customer retention rate, the percentage of customers they kept from the year prior, was 80%. The year before, they had had 500 clients, and by retaining 80% of them, they kept 400. Next are the new customers. The company's conversion rate, the percentage of leads they converted into paying customers, was 10%. The previous year, Suburban's marketing efforts generated 500 leads, and by converting 10% of them, they got 50 new paying customers. That is how they got a total of 450 customers for the year.

Next, let's examine Suburban's average spend, which is a function of how many times per year their customers buy their services and how much they spend each time. Suburban's clients bought the company's services on average twice a year and spent on average $2,000 each time, which multiplies to the average spend of $4,000 per year. When we multiply the average spend with the 450 customers, we come back to where we began, which was $1.8 million in sales. Now we have identified the five levers, retention rate, lead generation, conversion rate, average spend, and gross profit rate, which was 40%. All these combined generated the gross profit of $720,000. Subtracting the expenses of $600,000 left Suburban with the profit of $120,000.

5 Levers Analysis - Suburban Management

	Current
Last Year Count	500
x Retention Rate	80%
Repeat Customers	400
Leads	500
x Conversion Rate	10%
New Customers	50
# Customers	450
x Average Spend	4,000
Sales	1,800,000
x Gross Profit %	40%
Gross Profit	720,000
Expenses	600,000
Profit	120,000

Figure 4-2, Suburban Management 5 Levers Analysis.

Now that we have isolated our five levers, we can see the result of improving each of them by applying the systems that you will learn in the subsequent chapters in this book. Let's begin with the retention rate. By keeping more of their existing customers,

Suburban's retention rate would increase. They implemented a loyalty system, a customer feedback system, and a skill development training system for their team. By doing so, they improved their retention rate by 8%, making their new retention rate 88%. After applying a similar approach to systemize their lead generation and improve their conversion rate, they increased their number of leads from 500 to 550 and increased their conversion rate by 1%, making their new conversion rate 11%. They could increase the average spend three ways: They could do it by improving the frequency with which their customers bought from them, they could do it by increasing the amount they spent each time, or both. By establishing systems for regular service appointment scheduling that resulted in more frequent visits, they achieved a 10% lift in average spend. They also improved the components of the gross profit rate—price and cost—and were able to increase it from 40% to 44%.

Let's look at the impact of those changes. With a new retention rate of 88%, they were able to repeat business with 440 of the 500 customers they had the prior year. Their improved lead generation and conversion rate increased their number of new customers to 61. That added up to 501 customers served in total. The increased average spend of $4,400 brought the revenue from $1.8 million to about $2.2 million. With the improved gross profit rate of 44%, they got a gross profit of $970,000. Unfortunately, it's difficult to hold expenses down when growing a business, so Suburban budgeted their expenses to increase 10% from $600,000 to $660,000. A gross profit of $970,000 minus expenses of $660,000 yielded $310,000. As you can see, Suburban was able to more than double their profit from $120,000 to $310,000 by breaking down their business model into its constituent levers and then influencing each of those levers systematically to achieve a dramatic change in profit and, as a result, in the value of the business itself.

5 Levers Analysis - Suburban Management

	Current	Improvement	Systemized
Last Year Count	500		500
x Retention Rate	80%	7%	86%
Repeat Customers	400		428
Leads	500	7%	535
x Conversion Rate	10%	7%	11%
New Customers	50		57
# Customers	450		485
x Average Spend	4,000	7%	4,280
Sales	1,800,000		2,076,849
x Gross Profit %	40%		43%
Gross Profit	720,000	7%	888,891
Expenses	600,000		642,000
Profit	120,000	7%	246,891

Figure 4-3, Suburban Management 5 Levers Analysis

By now you should have a clear sense of your *why* to kick off your systemization plan. You have seen the kind of profit lift you can achieve by making incremental improvements in the systems that sustain your business. And the benefits go beyond that to the quality of your life and those around you. It takes persistence and patience to get there, so the sooner you get started, the sooner you will arrive at your destination and enjoy the fruits of your labor.

In Part 2, you will learn how to go about setting up the essential systems. These are the ones that have been proven to have the most benefit for the investment of work required to get them started. Let's get started.

PART 2

The Perfect Business Framework: Implementing The 9 Systems

CHAPTER 5

Self-Management

Does this sound like your day? You are deep in work, and then you look up the clock and say, "Oh no, I've got to get to the parent–teacher conference that started five minutes ago!" You scramble to pack up and run out the door because you were just so busy reacting to emails, phone calls, interruptions, and crises of one sort or another that you lost track of time. Perhaps you forgot to get lunch even though you managed to get sucked into checking your stock quotes on your phone every 15 minutes. The day just flew by, and as you are driving to the conference, you ask yourself, "Where did the day go?"

Well, that is not unusual. It's common for owners to be not only a focal point in the business but also a bottleneck just because of the sheer volume of communication that has to flow through them. It can become overwhelming very quickly. Of course, the things we don't like, we avoid, so we tend to push them back. For example, we easily push aside bigger, long-term projects like creating a new system for the business, and then it's easy to lose track of details, which leads to mistakes or missed opportunities. Instead, we may spend our time on things that are *urgent* but not really *important.*

High-performing owners, those who have figured it out, are focused and disciplined and seem to get a lot more done than others. You can become that kind of owner with some education and the right tools and by building a few simple habits. Here's how you can systemize your approach to your day to become more effective with less effort.

FIVE KEYS TO HIGH PERFORMANCE LEADERSHIP

There are five keys you need to implement to become a high-performing owner—*clarifying the big picture, sustaining focus, using leverage, controlling the environment,* and *using tools rather than muscles.*

Clarify the big picture. You wouldn't take your family on a vacation trip in your car without knowing where you're going. You would choose the destination and plan the route. You wouldn't just drive randomly until you found somewhere you liked. If you did that, what would happen? You would never get there. Nevertheless, many business owners run their business this way. They don't have a clear direction of where they are going; they just run very hard trying to get there. As a result, they get nowhere fast.

Right now, can you say exactly what you are building? Can you paint a crystal-clear picture of it in words?

I once posed those questions to a pair of brothers, Dan and Frank, who were co-owners of an office technology company that they had inherited from their father. I asked them, "Where do you want to go? What are you building? What does it look like when it's finished?" Dan, not having thought about it very much, stumbled around but eventually landed on, "Well, I'd like the company to be $20 million." This took Frank completely by surprise. Although he hadn't thought of it much, his brother's wishes in terms of the size and scope were completely different from his own. He looked at Dan and asked, "Why do we need all of that? Why would we want all of those employees and all those headaches?" We were able to resolve the conflict of interests, but the point is that even though they had been working side-by-side for 10 years, they had never gotten on the same page about what they were trying to accomplish together.

No vision of your future means there can't be any clear goals for the team or any sense of connection to the journey, nor any sense of how to get there because you don't know where you are going. It's time to get clear on your big picture. Make some decisions and determine what you want. It will help you at the daily and even the hourly level when you are prioritizing your tasks and deciding where to allocate your time.

Sustain focus. Humans can focus their attention on a task for approximately 20 minutes. That is about it. Bright, shiny objects will distract from that. If you try to draw back from the 20 minutes up to a day, a week, a month, a quarter, or even a year, it's easy to see why the goal you set at the beginning of the year tends to be forgotten and left by the side of the road along the way.

Focus requires discipline, but that is exactly what many entrepreneurs lack. You need some active course correction to retain and sustain the focus. Luckily, you can let your subconscious mind do some of the work for you. Your habits determine most of your behavior, so put them to work.

Forming habits does take some time, though, and you can't rely on that alone. You need to find a way to constantly remind yourself of what is most important so you can plan how you are going to get there. That requires some planning time. There is an old saying that a woodsman was once asked, "What would you do

55

if you had just five minutes to chop down a tree?" He answered, "I would spend the first two and a half minutes sharpening my ax." It doesn't take much to incorporate planning time every day in order to focus your attention on the right things and keep your mindset in good shape for maximum performance. Thinking you don't have time to do your planning is a sign that you need it badly.

Use leverage. Here leverage refers to getting things done by doing less of the work that you can accomplish by other means. Other means might be one of several things. It could be automation through technology. It could be delegating work to someone either inside or outside the company. Or it could be stopping doing it altogether because it's not important or urgent.

As an owner, you probably have a high capacity for work, or you wouldn't be in business. That can work against you when you believe that the answer whenever you get overwhelmed is more hard work. What you need to do is look at exactly how you are spending your minutes and compare that to how you want to be spending your minutes. Then analyze what you can delegate without worrying exactly how just yet. You can cut back the work that can be done by somebody else or some other way at a lower expense. You need to build a delegation plan to peel off those tasks from you and find another way to get them done.

Control the environment. When you were in high school, there was a schedule to follow. The bell rang, and you went into the classroom and studied, say, chemistry. Now, you didn't study chemistry until you were done learning everything there was to learn about it; you just studied it until the next bell rang, and then you left the classroom. Without the schedule, there would be no results whatsoever in the entire high school. The schedule helped all the students and teachers to accomplish the goals. You can apply the same principle to your day by controlling the environment around you to support the goals that your naturally wandering mind doesn't want to handle. Set up your own class schedule by using your calendar. Systemize your day in line with your priorities to stay on track on a minute-to-minute basis by setting aside chunks of time to do the most important things.

Use tools, not "muscle." No matter how much you plan, things that you didn't expect will come at you. There is a flood of daily tasks, interruptions, and other crises that are just too much for your brain to keep track of by itself. That is why you want to use tools, not your muscle (your mind muscle, that is) and systemize your task management. Whatever system you choose needs to be dynamic because it must be able to keep track of things so that nothing slips through the cracks.

The Performance Formula

Performance = Attention x Persistence

Figure 5-1, Performance Formula.

To summarize, you can see that your performance is a function of your attention and persistence. That is the formula for performance. The formula applies not just to you, but to your business as well. Performance requires attention, a focus on the most important things that will make you effective—your big goals (for example, all the systemization projects you undertake), but it also requires the persistence to stay on them and drive them to conclusion. The tools I will share with you later support the twin drivers of attention and persistence by setting and sustaining them. We will follow the systematization approach of prioritizing, analyzing, optimizing, and institutionalizing, in this case for managing yourself in addition to your business.

THE FIVE SYSTEMS OF SELF-MANAGEMENT

There are several systems you can implement right away—a *destination plan*, a *daily self-management session,* a *personal delegation plan*, a *time blocking system*, and a *task management system*. Here's how to get them started.

Destination plan. The only way to get clear on your personal vision for you and your business is to write it down. If it isn't on paper, it doesn't exist. So grab a pen and a tablet of paper, sit down in a quiet place without interruption, and write the answers to the following questions about your future completed business. Think about it in its future state—as it will exist five years from now:

1. Why does your business exist? In other words, what problem do you solve and who do you solve it for?
2. What is the annual revenue?
3. What does the physical space look like? Describe it in detail, including the sights, sounds, and feelings you get when you walk through the door.
4. How many people are on the team?
5. What is it like to work there for your team? Describe the culture.
6. How do you want to be perceived in the marketplace by your customers? How do you want to be perceived by your competitors?
7. What words would you use to describe your employees' characteristics?
8. How would you describe the customers you serve?
9. What experience do they get when they interact with you and your business?
10. How many hours a week do you work?
11. What is your day-to-day role in the business?
12. What does your management team look like?

13. How much profit do you make and how much of it is distributed to you?
14. How does the business serve your personal goals?

Write in as much detail as possible and read it aloud when you are finished. If it doesn't get you excited, something is wrong.

Daily self-management session. The daily self-management session is how you begin your day, either at home or the office, before anyone can disturb you. It prepares you for the day ahead by forcing you to stop, think, and regain perspective and motivation. Everyone has a different twist on this technique. Here is one that synthesizes the best practices you may have heard about from others that you can adapt for your use. This will take about 10 or 20 minutes—it's up to you to find the right timeframe for you.

Sit down with your agenda and write the answers to the following questions and follow the steps:

1. What are you committed to right now? (This week's goal.)
2. What are you most excited about right now?
3. What are three new things for which you are grateful?
4. What are yesterday's top three accomplishments?
5. Prioritize:
   a. Review your quarterly plan (which will be explained later).
   b. What are the top five things you are most concerned about completing right now?
   c. Which one thing from the list would bring the most satisfaction if you completed it today?
6. Choose one item from the list above and make that your focus for the day.
7. Take 20 minutes to think about problems you need to solve.
8. Set up your calendar for the day to include time to accomplish your one most important thing from above.

It will take you time to develop this process and habit, but you will see results in terms of your effectiveness right away. The preset agenda makes it easy to do.

Personal delegation plan. Follow the systematization approach described earlier (prioritize, analyze, optimize, institutionalize) to implement this system. First get an understanding of exactly how you are spending your time by writing down all of your work activities. If you struggle to do this, commit to logging your activities by the task for one or two representative weeks to get a clear picture of how you are investing your time. Then categorize your activities on the two criteria *skill* and *desire* in the sorter sheet below.

Personal Delegation Plan Sorter

Skill		
High	Estimating Responding to Complaints Screening candidates Reviewing financials	Planning Designing new marketing Interviewing candidates Building systems
Low	Reviewing invoices Travel arrangements Arranging meetings Collections	Ordering material Reviewing sales orders Sorting through emails Scheduling work
	Low High	

Desire

Figure 5-2, The Personal Delegation Plan sorter sheet.

Congratulations, you have just created your delegation plan. Start by looking into how you can get the "low-low" rated tasks done without doing them yourself but rather delegating them (either internally or by outsourcing them), automating them, or just quit doing them if they are duplicate efforts.

You also may have created a job description for your future personal assistant. If there are many "low-low" tasks, there might be enough work to take on a personal assistant full-time. When is the right time to bring in a personal assistant? If you are asking the question, it's probably yesterday. Ask a friend who has one when the right time to hire is. They will probably tell you the same thing—that yesterday is the right time.

Keep working through the list one task at a time to get a sense of freedom that you haven't experienced before. You will never run out of things to delegate; just start chopping up the higher-level tasks into smaller pieces, and you will find plenty of opportunities to free yourself from more and more of your day-to-day work.

Time blocking system. The time blocking system gives your most important tasks a place to live in your calendar. If you don't use this system, the forces that compete for your attention will win the battle for your attention and focus, and the most important projects will not get the focus you want to give them.

Begin by designing your calendar the way you want each day of the week to happen. Start with the weekly commitments you have to keep, like team meetings or any standing one-on-one meetings. Then place in one-hour blocks during which you can focus on your most important but not urgent goals for the week, essentially setting appointments with yourself. Leave gaps to handle the normal chaos that ensues plus your remaining ordinary workflow.

Now you have a default plan for every hour of your day that you can follow. It may not survive the crises that tend to happen, but it will tell you exactly where to go each next hour of your day since you have set aside time for the big-picture tasks that you want to accomplish. It has the added benefit of forcing you to think about delegation. When you put all your activities down on paper and see how much work there is to do, at a certain point, you will see that there is only one solution to getting it all done, and that is to hire another person to help you get it done. This requires you to make a commitment to keep the appointments you make with yourself the same way you would keep an appointment with an important customer. You can work on your big-picture projects during the allocated time slots, but when the time is up, you stop and move on. It's just like the class bell ringing back in high school.

Task management system. Everyone has their own way of managing their day-to-day tasks. Some people rely on paper and pen, while others rely on their computers or cell phones. Either way works. Choose the one that suits you the best, adopt it, and adapt it to your personal preference. The system works with any tool you choose.

The task management system is dynamic and requires attention two ways. Every day, you'll need to set it up. You can do that in your daily self-management session. And approximately every hour or so, as you go through the work throughout the day, you'll need to refresh your task prioritization, because things change throughout the day.

Inspired by the One Minute To-Do List by Michael Linenberger (you can learn more from him), here is an 80/20 version of the system that you can use to manage your task: On paper, in your task manager on your Outlook, or on your cell phone, divide your tasks into the following three separate categories:

1. Today's tasks—the tasks that must be done before you go home today. Limit it to five items.
2. This week's task—the tasks that must be done between the next day and seven days out. Limit it to 20 items.
3. This month's tasks—the tasks that can be started greater than seven days from today.

Here is what you do with the tasks in each of the three categories:

1. Today's tasks: Review the five tasks approximately once every hour throughout your day. They may shift around as you complete some of them and new ones come up. Although you may need to shift around the top five items, you never should have more than five.
2. This week's tasks: Review the 20 tasks each morning, and decide what you want to add or subtract. Move the ones you subtract to the list of this month's tasks.
3. This month's tasks: Review the tasks about once a week.

Your tasks and priorities change throughout the day, and you probably will have a sense of urgency regarding the most recent things. The task management system helps you keep the most important items near the top.

When you list the tasks, write down only the next steps, not broad projects. For example, instead of writing, "Do all my performance reviews," simply write, "Set the dates for the performance reviews" if that is the next step in that process.

Done all together, these systems take away the power of your mind's natural tendencies to wander and replace them with structure and habits that will serve you well and set the tone for the rest of your team.

CHAPTER 6

Culture

The culture in your company has a tremendous impact on your results. It is also the most difficult thing to work on because it is so abstract. Trying to understand or influence the culture is like trying to nail Jell-O to the wall. It's important, though, because either it serves you or it works against you in achieving the goals of the business.

If you ever have thought that your employees don't care about anything, don't understand, aren't happy no matter what you do, don't have the same urgency that you do, or have a plain bad morale, I can promise you that it is coming through in their communication to your customers and that it's costing you in lost opportunity, lost profit, and mistakes. You have a lot on the line. Your future depends on keeping your customers happy, and if the team isn't happy, they won't serve the customers well. So you need to create an environment that makes your team want to be proactive and independent within the boundaries of their roles, one that encourages them to use good judgment and act like owners because when everyone has the same attitude and a clear goal, you have a competitive advantage. That advantage will express itself in the way you recruit and retain your team and the sense of ownership throughout the organization. It results in a superior experience for your customers and team and a much more enjoyable environment where you spend the bulk of your time.

HOW CULTURE WORKS AND AFFECTS YOUR BUSINESS

To understand how to master the culture and make it serve you, you have to understand its effect and how it works. Every company is a community, which means it has norms—group expectations of behavior. These norms are often supported by peer pressure. It's a self-sustaining system of traditions, customs, patterns of practice, or behavior that are built over time.

Many norms are unspoken; they are learned through observation of other people or cause and effect. For example, if someone sees their boss leave work at 3:55 every day, no matter what, they will naturally develop a similar habit. They are rewarded with an easy last half hour of work and not having to beat the traffic home, so their life is good. No one trained them explicitly to leave at 3:55, but through trial and error and observation, they will learn and became conditioned to do that.

Other norms are more explicit or formalized. They come from the processes that have their own cause and effect on them such as the way you compensate or incentivize. For example, if you pay a bonus for sales every month, what is going to happen on the last day of the month? Sales will often get jammed into the system, and the quality of those sales tends to go down as well because people are trying to beat a deadline. The norms may also come from rewards such as face time with the boss, promotions, and recognition. In some organizations, sales is king, and the production team resents that sales receives all the love.

Norms can also include values—what is important to you and the organization. Values can be unspoken as well, which means they are learned by the tribal method, and that is often the case. They can also be more formalized: explicitly defined. If they aren't explicitly defined, they will change as players come and go in the organization. With each new player who joins the team, the values can shift and change according to the personalities involved. Your intended values become diluted, and eventually, they may no longer reflect the values you wanted when you started the business.

Norms guide our thinking and attitudes, positive as well as negative. They guide and influence the decisions and choices we make. Our thinking, attitudes, and decisions all determine our actions, including how we communicate inside and outside the organization, how we interact with the systems, and how we use judgment for better or worse. All those things drive behaviors, and it's those behaviors that in turn drive the results. You see the results in the form of profit; the team's engagement, morale, and attention; the recruiting; the consistency or lack thereof in quality; the customer satisfaction; and the predictability of the business.

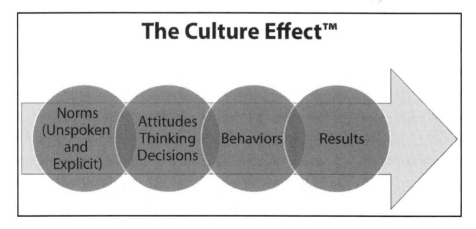

Figure 6-1, The Culture Effect.

Here is an example of how the culture can express itself in your business. Say you receive a customer complaint. Your customer didn't get the shipment they demanded and expected on Monday. That was the result. When you ask why it happened, you discover that Jimmy, the shipping manager, didn't send out the shipment on Friday, even though it was ready and there was nothing standing in the way of getting it out. That was the behavior he exhibited. You ask why he didn't do it, and you learn that it was because he left early without thinking about completing the shipment. That was the thinking that drove his behavior. "Why?" you ask again. You find that there was no sense of urgency. That was the norm that was taught to Jimmy. It wasn't a shortage of materials, a back-ordered part, or a logistical obstacle that caused Jimmy not to complete the shipment on Friday; it was simply his lack of urgency.

To change the result, you first have to look at the system. If the system is sound, and it was followed, you can look at the behaviors that produced the result. Once you do that, you can diagnose the attitudes, thinking, and decisions that produced that particular behavior. Then you can look underneath for the norms, either unspoken or explicit, that produced those attitudes, thinking, and decisions. As it turns out, Jimmy's boss wasn't too concerned about getting the shipment sent out on Friday. He figured it could go out on Monday, no big deal. Jimmy adopted his boss' attitude. The norm they created between them was one of no urgency, and Jimmy was influenced by this unspoken agreement about how things were done, so he behaved just as you would expect. This tacit understanding was an element of the culture. So, to affect the culture, you need to influence the norms that constitute it.

THE FIVE UNIVERSAL NEEDS AND DESIGNING THE CULTURE YOU WANT

When designing your culture, there are five universal needs that you have to consider to establish its effectiveness and systemize it to keep it the way you want.

People need clarity. Values help provide clarity. Define your values so they can be guideposts for your employees' behavior and decision making in your absence. The values can't be so vague that your employees don't get the connection to their daily work activities. They need to be practical and concrete.

Here's an example of how simple this can be. In the office of a garbage hauling business somewhere in Maryland, there is an old piece of cardboard nailed to the wall. Written on it in black magic marker are 12 short sentences that comprise the rules of their culture. They don't call it that, but that is what it is. It says things like, "If you show up late, you are fired" and "If you finish early, you can go home." Even something as simple as that has the benefit of being concrete and completely understandable to the entire team. The values need to provide this kind of guidance. In other words, just using the word *honesty* as a value is not very effective. It's much more effective to say, "We will never promise a delivery date that we aren't certain we can meet, even if it means losing an opportunity." That is a statement that everyone can connect to, understand, and follow without confusion every day.

People need independence. Well-defined values or principles give some guidance to the independence that people need. They also encourage an appropriate level of risk-taking, so employees can use them as a standard against which they can make decisions that are outside the norm of their day-to-day routine.

People need to know where they stand. If your employees don't know the score of the game, they can't tell if they are winning or losing, so give them the score. It would include the score for the performance of the company, their department, and especially, them personally. Knowing that will help them become more productive and engaged in their work.

People need connection. They want to be part of something bigger than themselves—from their relationships with the team to their relationship with the company, so make it worth belonging to and show them that their connection has a higher purpose.

People need recognition. They perform better when they are motivated, and recognition increases that motivation. For that reason, you need to design a system where performance is recognized so that it increases motivation and, in turn, spurs higher levels of performance. It's a virtuous cycle that builds motivation. It is fueled by the systems you put in place to ensure a frequent and steady dose of recognition for the performance you desire. Human psychology does the rest.

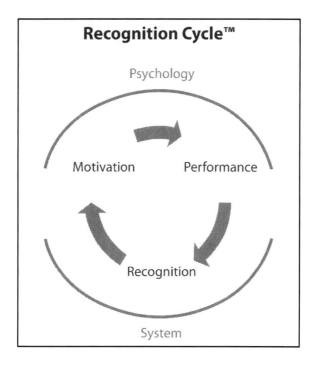

Figure 6-2, The Recognition Cycle.

SYSTEMS FOR INFLUENCING THE NORMS

Before implementing systems to change the norms in your company, define your values or principles by which you conduct business. Be specific. Gather together your key players, and clearly describe the behaviors of your star employees. Then use those descriptions as models for your values. You can also use the founders' stories or beliefs or past stories of success to create clearly defined principles. Limit the number of principles or values to between five and 10, and then establish them as the guidelines for how you expect your team to behave and how they make decisions—how you do business.

Now let's look at some systems you can use to influence the cultural norms in your team. We will focus on *recognition systems* and *communication systems*.

Recognition systems. One formalized recognition system you can establish is an awards program. When designing such a program, remember that it's not about money; it's about the recognition, so it doesn't have to be an expensive activity to be effective. Base the awards on objective criteria, enforce the deadlines (don't miss them), and give the rewards in public.

Another recognition system you can use that has a magical effect is handwritten notes—for birthdays, for work anniversaries, or just to say thank you. So take the time to write personal notes to your employees. Be specific. For example, when you write a thank-you note, take the time to describe the exact behavior that caused you to be grateful to them. Then connect that specific behavior to the overall vision of the company, and express your gratitude. Send the notes to your employees' homes so they can share them with their families and can keep them. Then they become powerful motivators for them. Just don't use email, please. It doesn't have the same effect.

A third traditional recognition system is some kind of instant celebration ritual to do when something good happens. The classic example here is a bell that someone gets to ring when they make a big sale.

Peer-based systems also work well. One of my clients has created a system where, at every monthly meeting, one of the employees gives a prize to any other employee in the company who they think has gone above and beyond the call of duty. The recipient of the prize not only gets the recognition and a gift card; they also have an obligation to give the award to someone else in the company at the next meeting. So the award system continues, meeting to meeting, driven by each recipient of the award.

Since people love contests, you can also align whatever objectively measurable short-term goals you have to specific prizes and then award the achievement of those goals in public. The contests don't have to be limited to sales. They can be focused on any particular measurement or activity that leads to a measurable desired outcome.

Involving the team in process development and process improvement is in itself a powerful motivator and a way to affect the norms in the business. When the team is involved in the solution, it causes continuous improvement thinking.

You could also set up a system where the prize in a contest or the recognition for some achievement is lunch with the president. Sam Walton of Walmart is famous for having lunch with the truck drivers on the shipping dock whenever he went to visit a store. He didn't do it just to make the truck drivers feel good; he also did it to learn from them. That became a recognized habit that the rest of his managers took up as they grew the business.

Communication systems. Whenever I conduct a team survey, the most common response I get to questions about ways to improve has one common theme: communication. There never seems to be enough from the standpoint of the team. There are lots of reasons contributing to this, but let's make sure you have the basics right. One example would be a weekly update on the wins and challenges of the past week in an email to everyone in the company, just to keep them informed about what is going on and recognize anything special that they do. Whenever you receive positive feedback from a customer, share it publicly via email or at a stand-up meeting. Annually, conduct state-of-the-company talks where everyone is gathered in one place, and you describe the performance, the vision for the coming year, and the challenges you face. There are plenty of opportunities to find a reason to communicate to the entire team.

Communication systems for new employees would include how you welcome them onto the team. Design a plan for their first day that goes beyond filling out forms and includes gathering everyone around to welcome them personally. Script out their onboarding with the right people and training resources to get off to a strong start. Set them up with a mentor to help them along.

Surveying your employees is another way of communicating with them. Simply by asking, you engage them more. It's easy to do this with the online services available today.

Share information about the financial performance of the organization with your employees. This idea causes a lot of apprehension for many entrepreneurs, but think about it: You can't expect your employees to improve their performance if they don't know the results of their efforts. Also, share and communicate with them key performance indicators and the priority of roles in the form of an accountability chart. We will discuss that further in the next chapter.

Above all, you must own the norms. Be a model by living the culture because as the captain of the ship, you have all eyes on you. Everyone on the team will scrutinize everything you do, so you must "walk your talk" if you want the rest of the team to play by the rules. Ownership does not confer upon you the right to take shortcuts or to ignore the rules of the game.

Many successful operators will tell you that culture eats strategy for lunch. That's because it is at the root of execution. You are the guardian of your culture and therefore are responsible for shaping it and upholding it.

CHAPTER 7

Performance Management

You know there's trouble coming when someone walks up to you and says, "I need to talk to you." It can seem like there isn't a day that goes by without some kind of people challenge—someone wants a bigger raise, someone else has an interpersonal conflict with a coworker or a personal issue that comes into the workplace. It can weigh on your mind, and it's easy to fall into the trap of saying to yourself, "I just can't find good people."

That's one reason why we build a performance management system. These are the systems that include everything related to your people—how you find them, choose them, integrate them into your team, lead and manage them throughout their career with your organization, and compensate them. Getting this right is important because there is nothing worse than a bad hire or an underperformer who drags down the rest of the team and causes good employees to leave.

Once your system is built, you can make smarter hires, and all the drama will decline. You will end up with a motivated team that is focused on results, and that is the path toward becoming the employer of choice in the eyes of prospective employees. Your costs are lower, your recruiting is a lot easier, and your retention is better because the systems remove the obstacles to satisfaction and give the employees the things they need.

FIVE GOALS OF THE PERFORMANCE MANAGEMENT SYSTEM

There are five goals that you need to design into the performance management system to make it effective—*clarity, results, alignment, discipline,* and *motivation.*

Clarity. Just as we discussed in Chapter 6, Culture, people want clarity in their roles and their responsibilities. They need to clearly understand the expectations about what they are supposed to do. Although that may sound simple and obvious, too many times I have walked into a business and asked someone what their role was or what their responsibilities were, and I have been met with a blank stare or a list of 12 or 13 different things that have no connection whatsoever to the workflow or the goals of the business. A lack of clarity pervades most organizations. This will remedy that.

Results. The performance management system, if properly designed, will help employees focus on results, not just activities, so they will be focused on doing the right things. It will have the effect of reducing training time for new employees, reducing cost, lowering the number of mistakes and delays, and in general producing more consistent results.

Alignment. As a business becomes more complex, every player has a more specific part of the workflow to fulfill. Unless they understand the importance and the context of their role, they will typically slide into their own comfort zones and work on other things that are less important, which will slow down the entire enterprise. A properly designed performance management system will align everyone's activities with the best route to the common goal.

Discipline. Systemization makes discipline happen. It brings about consistency. It reduces the need for improvisational decision making, and it speeds up the time it takes to make decisions. It prevents drama and misunderstandings, aligns expectations, and reduces surprises and unfairness in the team. It forces managers to manage rather than avoid conflict or neglect their duties of developing their people. It also subtracts emotions from the decision-making process. Life is a lot easier when everyone can rely more on predetermined policies to handle the routine types of decision making that happen every day in a business.

Motivation. You can improve performance and retention by boosting job satisfaction. If you can create an environment that fulfills the human psychological needs other than money, such as self-actualization, growth, and development through the strength of the systems, you will get higher job satisfaction and better performance in return.

THREE ELEMENTS OF THE PERFORMANCE MANAGEMENT SYSTEM

The performance management system consists of three elements: the *accountability plan*, the *key performance indicators*, and the *six fundamental performance management processes* that all support the goals of the performance management system in different ways.

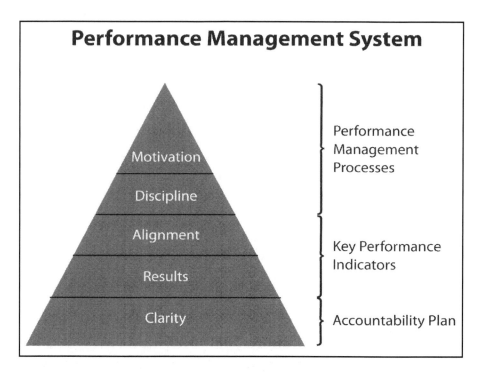

Figure 7-1, the Performance Management System model.

The accountability plan. The accountability plan is comprised of two components: the job description and the functional organization chart. Its purpose is to establish clarity in terms of responsibilities and lines of communication. The job description is the written description of what is expected of the employee. It includes a list of their specific duties and responsibilities and their key result areas and how these will be measured. It can also include characteristics or fundamental skills required for the job; other requirements for education, training, or physical requirements; and basic details such as reporting relationships, et cetera. A few key elements of the job descriptions are integrated into the functional organization chart, which is a diagram that shows each position and their hierarchical relationships. Included in each position box is a brief description of the top three to five key responsibilities for that role. It's a concise visual way to communicate clarity in terms of roles and responsibilities. The chart should be developed two ways: the current state, as it exists today, and the future state, which is a tool for planning and communicating with the team. It should be shared with the team so they can see the context of how they operate with everyone else. It's important that it is reviewed for updates periodically as people may come and go. Otherwise, it becomes outdated and loses its utility.

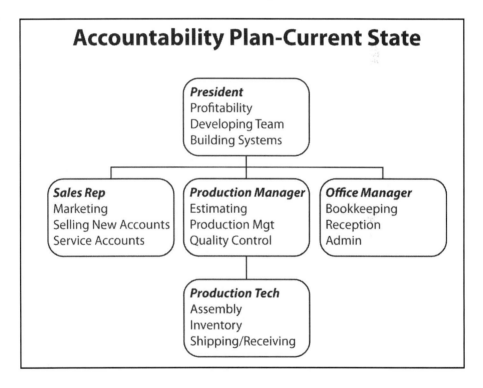

Figure 7-2, Accountability Plan – Current State.

Figure 7-3, Accountability Plan – Future State.

Key performance indicators. It's a cliché in management that, "If you can't measure it, you can't manage it." The key performance indicators (KPIs) are your measurement tool. As the numbers don't lie, they are an objective source of evidence that you can use to measure and communicate productivity at all levels throughout the organization. They drive sound decisions based on evidence, not guesses, and make decision making faster and easier, especially when things are very busy and the owners are buried in work. They are important also because small changes in critical levers in the business can make big differences in profit. They help the team focus on getting results, and if they are designed properly, they will bring about alignment between each team member and the bigger goals of the company. Monitoring them will show you exactly what is working at all levels of the business and what needs to be fixed. Trying to run a company without them is like flying an airplane without any working instruments, at night, in the fog.

KPIs measure productivity, or throughput, which can be expressed as units of results divided by a unit of resource. For example, one measure of the sales conversion rate would be the number of sales won divided by the number of proposals presented. It's a measurement you can use to diagnose the effectiveness of your sales process and pricing strategy. If it's too high, there might be room to increase the prices. If it's too low, there could be a price issue, but it also could signal some other things. The key is to understand the way it's trending and why it's trending that way.

A more predictive KPI for sales effectiveness would be the number of face-to-face meetings with prospects held per week. Since meetings are a predictor of the number of proposals created, and proposals, in turn, predict the resulting sales, a measure of the frequency of face-to-face meetings will tip you off to a change before it shows up on the sales report. You could think of that as a *key predictive indicator* in addition to the key performance indicator.

You can measure anything. For example, you can measure culture, a measure of which would be an employee satisfaction index. Or you can measure the strength of the culture by measuring the voluntary termination rate. Though it might seem difficult, there is a way to measure just about anything that is happening in a business.

For each box on the functional organization chart, and for each department, the question is, what is their goal, and how can you best measure it? Choose activities that are predictive of the larger goals like the face-to-face meetings. Make sure that the measurements are objective and measurable. The KPIs also need to be actionable. In other words, they need to be possible to influence by whoever is being measured. Lastly, it's important to focus on the few most important activities. More than three or four KPIs for a person will cause diffusion in focus and inability to produce significant results in any one area.

When you go about determining KPIs in your business, ask how you would know you are successfully accomplishing that particular role or task, and what the best measure for that is. Then you can set up the measurement system and start reporting the results. It's important to keep it simple. Ideally, you can display the results in a graphical format for ease of interpretation. After measuring for a while, you will be able to determine a baseline from which you can act on it and proceed to improve it step by step.

Performance management processes. There are six basic performance management processes to install: *recruiting, selection, training and development, performance evaluation, compensation,* and *performance improvement.*

Figure 7-4, Performance Management Processes.

Recruiting. Recruiting for a new role is like marketing. Just like you need to have a clear picture of your target customer, you need to know clearly who your target candidate is. The best way to identify what you are looking for is to look at the duties, responsibilities, and characteristics of the ideal team player that you listed in the job description you created. Then you can design your advertisement based on that. Look for the right behavioral attributes first and vocational skills second because the former are much more difficult to change than the latter.

In addition to the traditional advertising routes for finding new candidates, there are some other tactics you need to employ to cast a wider net to find the highest number of qualified candidates for the job. The first tactic is to ask your employees for referrals. As your employees already know the culture and what it's like to work there and the requirements of the job, their referrals are usually highly qualified candidates. Whoever they are willing to extend their credibility to refer should immediately get onto the list for consideration. You can stimulate employee referrals by setting up a rewards system for successful referrals. Your customers are also good resources for candidates. Like your employees, they already know you, so asking them for referrals usually will result in a few qualified candidates. During recruiting, everyone in the organization should modify their email signatures to mention that the company is looking for a new player and a brief description of whom you are looking for. Social media is a great resource for attracting qualified candidates as well. Set up ad templates that you can pull out whenever you need them. Then fill in the data from your job description. Depending on your needs, it might be best to recruit consistently. If you frequently look for people, keep the recruiting going so you always have a pool of candidates to draw from when the need arises.

Selection. Once you have a pool of candidates, you have to screen them by qualifying and interviewing them. Selection is how you bring in people and choose them for the team. I will now share with you a unique interview approach that condenses the timeframe you need and helps you makes higher quality decisions to choose the best candidates. It consists of two elements—an *interview panel* and specific *behavioral interviewing techniques* that go along with it.

The interview panel of three to four interviewers conducts all the required interviews in one specifically formatted day. Involving several interviewers eliminates bias and forces consensus on hiring decisions to make better quality decisions that are based on evidence, not hunches. The interview process starts when all the candidates arrive at the same time in the morning. First, the candidates are given a group presentation about the company, the culture, the position, and what you are looking for in general. Then, throughout the morning, each interviewer conducts an approximately one-hour-long, one-on-one interview with each candidate. Depending on the number of candidates and interviewers, the process may extend into the afternoon. The same day, or as soon as possible, the panel gathers to compare notes, judge the candidates on the specific desired attributes, and decide which candidate to recommend.

The process relies on behavioral interviewing techniques—specific ways of questioning to elicit past behavior that is predictive of future behavior. It's important to master these techniques for several reasons. For one, history repeats itself. The best predictor of someone's behavior tomorrow is how they behaved yesterday. These questioning techniques are designed to uncover stories and evidence from the interviewee's past that will shed light on how they are likely to behave as your employee. It's also important because attributes trump skills. Attributes are much more difficult to change than skills, which can be trained. If you understand the attributes you need, and you can find them in the candidate, you are much more likely to get a good fit than if you choose candidates based on skills alone. Remember that gut feelings are not evidence. You want to eliminate subjectivity and bring as much objectivity as possible to the process. It's also important not to mistake credentials for accomplishments. The questioning process will elicit accomplishments that will tell you much more about the candidate's likely performance than any credential they may have earned along the way.

It's imperative that you know what you want. You find that out by identifying the attributes of your ideal employee. Some examples of attributes you might look for are adaptability, energy, persuasiveness, communication skills, and human relations. When you have discovered what you want, you can build your behavioral questions around those key attributes. Then, in the questioning process, you will ask for direct evidence of past behavior that is related to each of your desired attributes.

There are several types of questions, two of which you want to avoid—hypothetical and leading, and one of which you want to focus on—behavioral. An example of a hypothetical question would be, "What would you do if a customer became abusive to you?" The candidate will answer that question the way they think you want to hear, so you won't learn much about what they really would do in that situation. An example of a leading question would be, "The last person in this job would break down completely when a customer became irate. Are you experienced with emotional situations?" When you ask that kind of question, you hand the answer to the candidate in advance, so you won't learn about what they would do with that either. To make the question behavioral, you would say, "Give me an example of a difficult customer you have dealt with recently. How did you handle the situation?" By asking this type of question, you force the candidate to think back to a concrete example that they can relate to you that will relay evidence about how they behave, which will tell you if they are who you are looking for. Other examples of behavioral questions would be, "Describe a situation where you went above and beyond the scope of your job to improve something," and "Tell me about a time when you strongly disagreed strongly with the actions your boss wanted to take. What did you do?" Just about any attribute you look for can be brought out by behavioral questions using the phrases, "Give me an example," "Describe a situation," or, "Tell me about a time when."

As you listen carefully to the candidate and probe, you need to pay attention to the story, which will consist of three parts: the *background* or context for the behavior you look for, the *action* that the candidate took, and the *result*—BAR.

Listening for Evidence

Background
Action
Result

Figure 7-5, Listening for Evidence.

Then take notes on their responses and rate to what extent the candidate's behaviors align with the specific attributes you want on a scale from 1 to 5.

After you and the other interviewers have interviewed every candidate, you meet to discuss your findings. You start with a blank score sheet. One manager will act as a scribe. You discuss and agree on overall ratings for each candidate and choose the right one. Then you will conclude with a recommendation, which includes verifying the candidate's references, conducting any further assessments, and making the offer.

The typical measure of effectiveness of hiring is judged by the likelihood that the new hire is at the company one year after they are hired. Without this approach, that likelihood is about 50%, which is no better than the flip of a coin. By following this system, you can increase it to well over 80%. It's worth the up-front effort to avoid the long-term pain of dealing with a bad hiring decision.

Training and development. The training and development (T&D) plan is a written document that describes how an employee will train and learn new skills. It spells out the activities they have to undertake to learn the new skills, where they can find the resources they need (a computer program, a training class, or someone else in the company), the deadlines by which they are expected to complete that activity, and how they will demonstrate their proficiency in the skills. The T&D plan can be used for improving an employee's performance, preparing them for a promotion, or cross training them, or it could be used for onboarding a new employee.

An example of one component of a T&D plan for a new sales administrator would look like this:

Activity: Convert specs into a proposal for a new customer.
Resource: Meet with a sales manager to learn how to read the specs and enter them into the proposal system and generate the finished proposal.
Deadline: Approximately one week.
Demonstration: Take a live sale from the spec sheet to a finished proposal in 30 minutes for the sales manager to review it.

The employee is responsible for taking ownership of executing their plan while checking in with their manager along the way to ensure that they are making progress and asking for help if it's needed.

Performance evaluation. In small businesses, performance evaluations are often non-existent. Sometimes they are informal, unstructured, subjective discussions that happen haphazardly. That's unfortunate because with a little planning, they can be a powerful tool to improve performance and develop employees.

In an effective performance evaluation, the reviewer evaluates two distinct perspectives of their direct report's performance: *what* they did and *how* they did it. What they did is the objective measurement of their results. It is expressed through their performance against the KPIs for the role. How they did it is more subjective. It can be based on the values of the business or other specific, agreed upon behavioral attributes. Above all, it has to be based on evidence—their specific results—and related to the attributes they are measured against, just like you would do in behavioral interviewing.

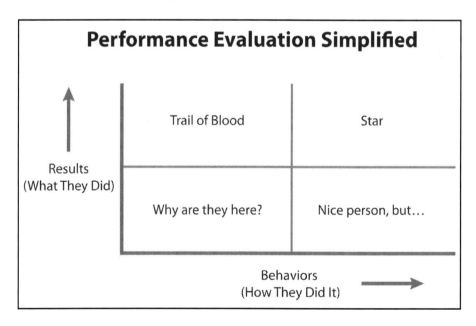

Figure 7-6, Performance Evaluation Simplified.

The performance evaluation process begins with a self-evaluation by the employee, after which the reviewer can compose and deliver the performance evaluation. The desired outcome is to clearly communicate a fair and comprehensive judgment of their performance along with specific goals for their continued growth and improvement supported by an appropriate training and development plan if needed.

As the employee will be overwhelmed with information and is likely to focus on the negative, since that is our natural tendency, the reviewer should conclude the evaluation with a headline that summarizes the overall message into one sentence that the employee can take away. Reviews are, by nature, retrospective; the subject of discussion is everything that has happened before the review. That does not help change your employee's behavior unless they receive the message in a way that sets expectations for future behavior. It's what Marshall Goldsmith would call "feed-forward." That is done by converting the headline into a concrete expectation of future behavior. It could be specific goals, a formal training and development plan, or just one simple thing.

For example, if the headline of your performance evaluation was, "Effective at doing the work but can be abrupt with customers," you can rephrase that in language that is forward-looking to communicate expectations. In this case, try, "Take your performance to the next level by slowing down and explaining your work to the customer clearly so you can give them a better experience."

With effective performance evaluation systems, evaluations will happen on a quarterly basis, but they can also take place semiannually or annually. They should all be conducted at once, not on the anniversary of employment of each employee because that is just too difficult to manage. Any discussion about pay changes should be separated from the performance evaluation and dealt with in another meeting. If the two subjects are blended together, the pay issue will preoccupy the employee's mind and will distract from the message you intended to deliver.

Once you commit to this process, it's important that the evaluations are done by the time you have said they would be because for an employee who is awaiting it, there is nothing worse than waiting longer than promised.

Compensation. Systemized businesses pay higher rates while spending less on their employment costs than other businesses. How is that possible? It's because these businesses tend to attract the best players, and they tend to pay the highest rates for those players, but since they are so well systemized, they require lower skills for each function than others, so they can pay more for the lower skill players. This also reduces turnover and its associated costs.

Let's look at how to handle base and incentive compensation.

In preparing base pay, it's best to base ranges on market rates and execute changes once per year, not on the anniversary of performance. This enables easy comparisons across the team to maintain fairness and condenses all the efforts to one period during the year, not sporadically throughout the year. Changes are based on performance in the context of the budget for the following year. It's typically best to do it at the beginning of the year.

When designing incentive compensation, you first want to think about what you are trying to accomplish by bringing it into the compensation program. The way bonus payments are determined is often a mystery to both the owner and the employee. Both sides wonder what the employee has to do to get the bonuses and how much they will be. Their expectations are often mismatched, and that results in frustration and disappointment. You can eliminate the frustration and disappointment by basing the bonuses on KPI objectives. The objectives and their associated incentive pay amounts can be based on individual performance criteria, company criteria, or a mix of both. Most businesses will opt for a blend, usually a ratio of 50/50 company to individual performance to calculate the payment amount. Company criteria may be a target number of profit or sales, and the payout is determined by performance.

Eligibility for receiving a bonus begins when the results meet a specific threshold, which is set at a certain percentage of the target results—usually 70 or 80% of target—and no bonus is paid for any result below that threshold. Likewise, they are capped at a maximum percentage above the target.

Individual criteria are based on the KPIs, and this payout has a threshold, target, and cap as well. The benefits of this system are that it is given to the employee in advance, it is transparent, it is objective, and it allows the employee to know where they stand at any time. As such, it prevents the employee from having false expectations regarding amounts or whether or not they will even receive a bonus. The payouts are typically annual, but quarterly payouts tend to be quite popular with employees because if their work is going badly at one point, these more frequent payouts allow for a fresh start every 90 days.

Performance improvement. The performance improvement system is important because it forces everyone to deal with performance issues in a timely manner. Underperformers can have a crippling effect on a small team, and owners or managers can avoid confronting them or take too long trying to turn them around. That can cause the team to start resenting the underperformers and blaming the owners or managers for tolerating the poor performance, and things may spiral downward. A systematic approach prevents this from happening.

Here is how the system works. First, if serious issues arise with an employee's performance, either in the results they get or how they get their results, document it. Warn the employee and explain why it's important. Document the discussion, and give them 30 days to correct it. If the employee hasn't taken any action within those 30 days, warn them again. This time, increase the level of seriousness to a written plan that states the specific expected behavior or performance and why it's important. It also needs to state the employee's specific behavior or performance that didn't meet that expectation. Now it's up to the employee to choose to leave the company or stay and commit to changing their behavior. If they choose to stay, they have to write out in a written plan exactly how they will change their behavior. To help the employee understand the consequences of not making amends, the written plan must also clearly state that failure to change may result in termination. Then set a review day 30 days out. After the 30 days, revisit the plan. If the employee still has not taken action, it's usually best to replace them. It's reasonable to do so because you have given them a fair chance to improve their performance and timely feedback along the way, and you have made the consequences clear if they fail to act.

All of this needs to be documented in the form of a handbook. A policy handbook will spare you from having to improvise in all the various situations that will come up with your employees throughout the year and make the likely outcomes clear to everyone in advance so that everything will run more smoothly.

CHAPTER 8

Finance

Although numbers are important, many owners hate them because the more you get into them, the more difficult it is to understand what they are telling you. This may cause a frustration that leads you to avoid them all together. Doing that is not good, though, because it results in unforeseen cash shortages that create uncertainties about the future, and that causes stress on you as the owner. Even if you pay close attention to your monthly profit and loss statement (P&L), you still don't know your future cash flow because the P&L is an instrument that looks backward, not forward. As a result, you live in fear of running short on cash. That causes you to make emotional decisions and underinvest in the business, which constrains growth.

Systemizing your numbers properly will enable you to see ahead and predict your future cash flow. It will also make the numbers easy to understand so you won't avoid using them. Most importantly, it will allow you to take specific actions to change outcomes before they develop into serious problems. Then you will no longer live in fear but instead be in control, able to make judgments based on evidence, not hunches.

WHAT YOU NEED TO KNOW TO PLAY THE GAME WELL

To play the game well, you have to know the score of the game. Imagine playing a basketball game with no scoreboard. You would have no idea if you were winning or losing the game or how much time there was left, so you wouldn't know whether you should stall or press or even sit on the bench and take a rest. Without the information from the scoreboard, you would just be going by your gut. That is what many business owners do. They run their businesses without knowing their sales, gross margins, profit, assets, liabilities, and all other key numbers. Knowing the score of the game is a beautiful thing because the numbers tell a story. They tell the truth in a pure, unemotional way without blame, excuse, or denial. Though they can be brutal, they allow you to make evidence-based decisions.

Also, be aware that small differences can make a big difference in outcomes. The application of the five levers model in Chapter 4 showed how slight changes in the critical drivers could double your profit. It works in reverse as well. The best example of this is discounts. Let's say you sell an hour of work that costs you $60 to produce for $90. That gives you a $30 gross profit. Then you decide to discount the hour of work by 10% from $90 to $81. The cost is still $60, so the gross profit shrinks to $21. Although the 10% discount is only $9, it is a 30% cut in your profit. In most businesses, that is the difference between profit and loss.

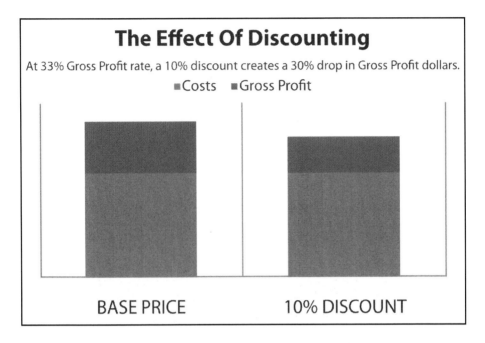

Figure 8-1, The Effect of Discounting.

The decision to give a discount is yours to make, but know that most erosion or leakage of profit happens in small amounts throughout the business. Knowing the numbers will enable you to break down each component so you can look into all those areas, control them where possible, and act to correct the problem or improve the results. When you make all the small, individual components of the business operate properly, the bigger results take care of themselves.

Lastly, you have to learn the language. There are three standard reports you need to understand: the *profit and loss statement*, the *balance sheet*, and the *statement of cash flows*. The profit and loss statement is like a movie, with a beginning and an end that tells you the story of how much profit you made over the course of a year or any other period. It doesn't tell you the whole story of how cash moves in and out of your business, though. For that, you need to understand your balance sheet. The balance sheet is like a snapshot of the financial condition of your business at a specific point in time. It's a financial picture of what you own, your assets, and how you financed them—either through debt or equity. Both the profit and loss statement and the balance sheet tell a part of the story of how cash moves in and out of your business.

The statement of cash flows ties the two together to explain the three ways cash moves in and out of your business on one page. The first of the three ways is *operating* cash flows. That is, like the profit and loss, the cash generated by the operations of the business. The second is *investing* cash flows. This would be cash used for the purchase of an asset, such as a new piece of equipment, or the cash generated by the sale of an asset. The third way cash moves in and out is through *financing*. This would be loans that you take on or pay off. It might also be additional equity investment or distributions of dividends to the owners. It's the most useful statement of the three to understand how your business generates and uses cash, but it's often the most neglected.

To get the full picture of your financial situation, you need to understand all three reports. Due to the effects of timing, "profit" does not equal "cash." This is why it can be confusing to see a profit on your P&L, but have a declining balance of cash at the same time. If you sell a product today, you might not get the cash from that sale until the invoice is paid 30 or 45 days later. As a result, the P&L by itself won't give you the true picture. For that, you need to look at all three, so it's important to build the habit of using these reports on a monthly basis.

As these three reports only look backward into the past, they can give you a false sense of security about the future. Running your business with this information only is like driving your car by looking in the rearview mirror. To understand where you are going and how you will get there, you need to begin looking through the windshield and focusing on what's ahead. The key indicators give you a picture of what will happen in your business in the time to come. They come in two forms: performance indicators and predictive indicators. The performance indicators are the financial analysis ratios, which tell you exactly how your business is performing today and give you a sense of the trend of the numbers based on recent history. The predictive indicator is your cash budget, which tells you where you are going. Projecting the future cash flows requires a sales forecast. When you have this information, you can take action. That's what's meant by the phrase "managing the business by the numbers" to profit. Then you can stop looking in the rearview mirror and instead look ahead.

SYSTEMS FOR SYSTEMIZING YOUR NUMBERS

We will now look at three critical systems that will help you understand where you are currently and where you are going: *financial controls, cash budgeting,* and *financial analysis.*

Financial Controls. The financial controls systems are simply the bookkeeping basics. Whether you operate these systems yourself or you have a bookkeeper operating them for you, you want to document them so that you aren't vulnerable to the loss of one person to keep your books in good order. Document how you do the following:

- Receive, process, and pay bills
- Create, transmit, collect, and process invoices
- Process payroll
- Reconcile bank accounts
- Other routine tasks.

It's best accomplished by getting the person who currently operates these systems to document them with checklists that are written to the level simple enough that a temp could step in and run them if they weren't there to do it.

The reporting of the three basic reports, the P&L, balance sheet, and statement of cash flows, along with your accounts receivable collections report, which summarizes what your customers owe you, has to be timely, accurate, and consistent for you to get the benefit of using them as you review them monthly.

Cash budgeting. The cash budgeting system displays your inflows and outflows of the operating, investing, and financial cash flows. Let's take a look at an example of a cash budget.

Cash Budget

	Jan	Feb	Mar	Apr
Cash Inflows				
Cash from Operations:				
Deposits Collected	80,000	125,000	200,000	150,000
Receivables Collected	85,000	100,000	150,000	100,000
Subtotal Cash from Operations	165,000	225,000	350,000	250,000
Cash from Other Sources:				
Extraordinary Items	-	-	-	-
New Borrowing ST	-	-	-	-
New Borrowing LT	35,000	-	-	-
Asset Sales	-	-	-	-
New Investment	-	-	-	-
Subtotal Cash Inflows	200,000	225,000	350,000	250,000
Cash Outflows				
Expenditures from Operations:				
Wages, Salaries, P/R Tax, etc.	90,000	90,000	135,000	90,000
Overhead Expenses	46,000	45,000	48,000	45,000
Payment of A/P for Mtrls/Subs	48,000	38,000	80,000	40,000
Other Operational Costs	1,000	1,000	1,000	1,000
Subtotal Expenditures from Operations	185,000	174,000	264,000	176,000
Other Expenditures:				
Extraordinary Items	-	-	-	-
Principal Repayment - LOC	-	-	-	-
Principal Repayment - LT	-	-	-	-
Payment of Other Liabilities	-	-	-	-
Asset Purchase	40,000	-	-	-
Distributions	-	-	-	45,000
Subtotal Cash Outflows	225,000	174,000	264,000	221,000
Net Cash Flow	(25,000)	51,000	86,000	29,000
Beginning Cash Balance	90,000	65,000	116,000	202,000
Ending Cash Balance	65,000	116,000	202,000	231,000

Figure 8-2, Cash Budget example.

As you can see, the cash budget divides the cash inflows from the outflows, and then it divides each of those into the categories described above.

In the category of cash inflows are the deposits and receivables you collect in a month, which give you the subtotal of cash from operations. Cash can come in from other sources as well. In this example, $35,000 of new borrowing long term comes in during the month of January. It represents a loan on a vehicle purchase. As such, it wouldn't necessarily show up in your P&L, but it is cash flow that you have to anticipate nevertheless.

In the category of cash outflows are wages, salaries, payroll taxes, overhead expenses, payments of accounts payable for things such as the cost of sales, materials, subcontractors, and labor related to that. These expenditures would show on your P&L, but there are other expenditures that wouldn't show there. In this example, you'll see $40,000 under asset purchase, which represents a vehicle financed by the $35,000 loan in the inflows above.

In this case, the inflows minus the outflows generate a negative $25,000 cash flow. In other words, you spent more than you took in during that particular month. The cash flow of the month combined with the beginning cash balance result in your ending cash balance, which is next month's beginning cash balance.

It's easy to predict your expenditures in the wages and salaries category, because they are more or less fixed, and your payments of accounts payable is just a function of how much you sell, so that is just a percentage of sales that you can calculate. So if you can forecast your cash inflows in the form of receivables, which is driven by your sales forecast, you can see what your cash flow will look like in the coming three, four, five, or six months.

Once built, it's not difficult or as time-consuming to update the cash budget each month along with your regular reports so that you can predict potential borrowing needs that may arise from seasonality or a downturn in business. You can use it to choose the best time to make any investments you need, like new equipment or new vehicles. And you can plan for distributions for tax payments or a dividend to the ownership to ensure you can afford them. This is the kind of control you can enjoy by setting up your forecast tools once and then simply operating them every month.

Financial analysis. Financial ratios are like the dials on a car dashboard. They come in different forms that give you information about your profitability, your liquidity, how efficiently you manage your business, and your financial return. There are many different types of ratios, but here are the first ones that I look for, the top five. First is the *gross margin*, which is defined as your sales minus cost of goods sold divided by sales. This ratio is the clearest and most controllable reflection of the value you create. As we saw earlier when we examined the five levers, it has a great impact on your bottom line. The second is the *quick ratio*, also known as the *acid test ratio*, which is your current assets minus inventory divided by current liabilities. It gives you a sense of how liquid you are and how readily you can pay your bills. Maintaining that ratio above 1 is critical to making sure you don't run short of cash. The *months of expenses coverage* is another important liquidity ratio. It is the amount of cash you have divided by your monthly general and administrative (G&A) expense. It gives you an idea of the cash balance you need to maintain so that you never run short. In terms of efficiency, the ratios *day sales outstanding* and *days payable outstanding* are key. The day sales outstanding ratio is a measurement of how long it takes you to collect your bills on average. To compute it, divide your accounts receivable balance by the last 12 months of sales and multiply that number by 365. That will give you the average number of days it takes you to collect your bills. The *days payable outstanding* is the average number of days it takes to pay your bills after receiving them. To compute it, divide your accounts payable balance by the last 12 months of cost of sales and multiply that by 365 days. The difference between the two represents what you will need to finance. The fastest and easiest way to become as efficient as possible from a financial perspective is to minimize your day sales outstanding (faster collections) and maximize your days payable outstanding (slower payments).

5 Key Financial Ratios

Gross Margin %	$\frac{\text{Sales-COGS}}{\text{Sales}}$	
Quick Ratio	$\frac{\text{Current Assets-Inventory}}{\text{Current Liabilities}}$	
Months of Expense Coverage	$\frac{\text{Cash}}{\text{Monthly G\&A Expense}}$	
Days Sales Outstanding	$\frac{\text{Accounts Receivable}}{\text{Trailing 12 Mos. Sales}}$	X 365
Days Payables Outstanding	$\frac{\text{Accounts Payable}}{\text{Trailing 12 Mos. Sales}}$	X 365

Figure 8-3, 5 Key Financial Ratios.

It's difficult to discern patterns or trends when looking at a table of figures. Looking at them graphically helps to understand the trends. Here is an example of a graph that displays the quick ratio (a measurement of your liquidity):

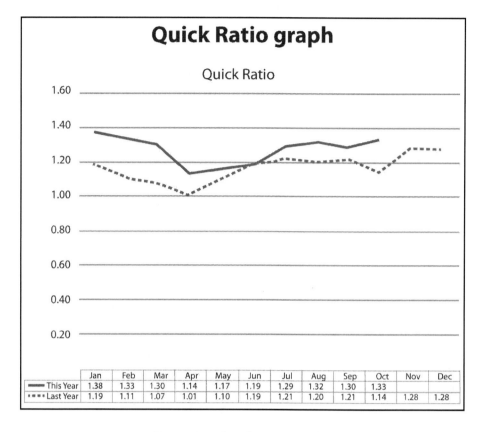

Figure 8-4, Quick Ratio Graph.

As you can see, it displays the ratio of the current year in a blue line against the ratio of last year in a dashed red line, month to month, over the entire last year. This kind of visualization allows you to detect trends more easily and anticipate changes well before they are likely to happen so you can take action.

A *cumulative* graph is an enhanced visual tool. Here is an example of a cumulative graph that illustrates year-to-date sales versus budgeted sales and last year's sales.

102

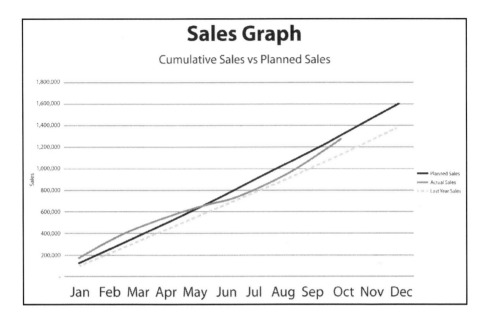

Figure 8-5, Cumulative Sales Graph.

This graph adds the sales every week and displays them on a line that looks like a mountain slope. The benefit of it is that the viewer can grasp the underlying trends and their implications easily and quickly. It shows the trend quite clearly against a reference, in this case, the planned sales (the black line) or against the performance from a prior period, in this case, last year's sales (the dashed orange line). It shows clearly when the current line dips below the goal, and clearly tells you that action is needed to get it back on target. It gives you a sense of context that you just can't get by looking at a table of numbers. The comparison period can be year over year, quarter over quarter, month over month, or even week over week.

When you get this kind of information out of your system, you can begin benchmarking—establishing specific thresholds or targets that will define good performance. That is a great thing to do if you can find good benchmarking data, but often it's difficult to come by. A lot of the information available for benchmarking purposes is no more than averages. The problem with using averages is that they are mediocre, and no business owner aspires to be that. So if you do get good information, it is useful for comparing your performance to your peers, but just be aware that the average of your peer's performance may be a poor representation of good financial performance. You need to focus on the top performers to judge your own performance. Even if you can't get good quality benchmarking data, your focus should be on improvement. At least set goals built on your budget or judgment about what is necessary to meet your business plan.

There are other basic indicators that you could graph to understand trends and activity detail in the business as well. We will go into those in upcoming chapters.

These are a few key ratios that I like to use. For a more thorough list of ratios that will give you a deeper understanding of your business, go to www.johnsheridan.com.

Installing the systems I have discussed in this chapter will improve your decision making and force you to look forward and anticipate problems before they become unmanageable. Better yet, they give you the information you need to make the small adjustments that can ratchet up your profitability.

CHAPTER 9

Execution

Steve, the second-generation owner of Safety Service Company, was frustrated with his team. They would have endless meetings, talking about everything they should do, and the ideas would flow like a river. Then they would all walk out the room and nothing would change. A month or two later, they would have the same meeting all over again, and someone would say, "Weren't we going to do that a while back? What happened?" Perhaps you have said this yourself. Few things are more frustrating for an owner than thinking you solved a problem only to have it happen again and again.

When I start working with a team, I ask them what the team could do better. Almost universally, the answer is communication, just like it was when I talked with the team at Safety Service. Although people associate the word with a lot of different things, they may use it to express their frustration with the flow of information or the kind of information they receive. I frequently hear a lot of talk about problem solving but see little follow through.

People see the problems that crop up repeatedly and realize that though they have solved those problems before, they haven't followed through on them. They also tend to lose track of their commitments, tasks, and priorities. Then they start wandering off course and find themselves in a rut, and the owner starts to wonder if it's the people who are the problems.

But if it's done right—if you can arrange it so that the team is made accountable, the big issues get the attention and focus they deserve, and the decisions that are made come to fruition—it brings confidence in the team's ability to turn decisions into actions and results.

Improving execution is a matter of creating new habits and forming systems that support the new habits. The good news is that it doesn't take a lot of money; it's all about disciplined management with the right tools and systems you are going to create.

KEY PRINCIPLES FOR THE EXECUTION SYSTEM

Let's take a look at the key principles underlying a successful execution system.

Direction—looking forward. You want to look forward and use predictive indicators. Choose ones that indicate what is likely to happen to get the outcome you want. For example, in the world of sales, leads lead to face-to-face meetings, the meetings lead to proposals, and proposals are required to make a sale. So if you just looked at sales, all you would see would be a lagging indicator. For predictive indicators that you can monitor to chart the future course of sales, you want to look at what's happening earlier in the sales process, like the flow of leads and number of meetings. Another example would be the way collections are managed. Typically, it's the customers who are over 90 days who get all the attention from the accounting team. But any customer who is over 90 days first had to get over 60 days, and any who is over 60 days first had to get over 30 days, so it's actually more effective to focus attention on those who trip over 30 days first. That way, you can be preventative in your communications and keep them from slipping to 60 or 90 days. Frequent monitoring of actionable indicators enables you to get commitments from the team to take the actions required to change the outcomes while there is still time and opportunity to do so.

Urgent vs. important. This is the daily battle for your attention in the course of day-to-day business. To offset urgency, you have to meet regularly. The typical objection here is, "We don't have time to do it" or "I've talked to them all day long. Why do we need to have another meeting?" Well, just because you are talking all day long doesn't mean that you are talking about the right things or that you are speaking about strategic issues or in the context of the most important goals of the company. What is important is the quality of your communication, not necessarily the quantity. To keep the focus on the important topics, you need to increase the frequency and regularity of the meetings.

Focus—less is more. Keep the main priorities in sight; otherwise, they will be lost in the chaos. As we discussed before, you want to set the right number of goals to prevent distraction. The organization will get distracted just as easily as you will if you have too many.

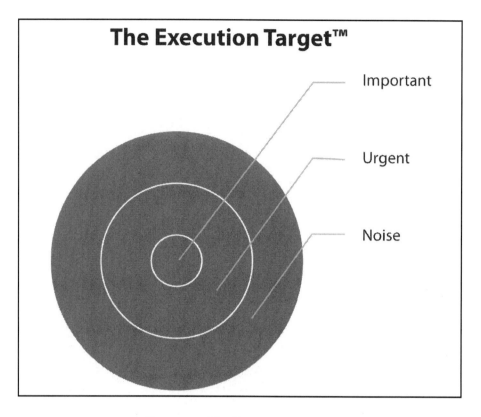

Figure 9-1, The Execution Target.

It's a lot like swimming in the open ocean versus swimming in a pool with lane markers. If you are plowing ahead with your head down in open water, you could be going in any direction unless you stop and take a look around once in a while and realign on your target. Whereas when you are in a swim lane, you can just feel the lane lines or watch the stripe on the bottom of the pool to keep going in the right direction. That is how the system works to keep you on track.

Accountability. The system will also bring about accountability. Accountability is an outcome. You need to set up the system to force the accountability drivers, which are the following:

- Transparency, removing any rocks that people can hide behind so everyone can see what their true behaviors and results are.
- Clarity, both in terms of the expectations everyone has of their performance and their ownership of different parts of the business.
- Objectivity, letting the numbers speak. As they don't lie, there is no lack of clarity around what the true results are
- Commitment.
- Peer pressure, using the power of the group to keep everyone on track
- Focus.

Rhythm. Rhythm is important for accommodating the natural human desire for consistency and forming the habits necessary to get the desired results. It maintains focus, prevents forgotten commitments, and helps you inspect your progress along the way.

SYSTEMS FOR EXECUTION

The execution systems are built around a rhythm of meetings at different intervals, beginning with annually, followed by quarterly, monthly, weekly, and daily, each with its own specific meeting and format and supported by tools. Annually, you will have a strategic planning day. Then on a quarterly basis, you will have a quarterly planning session and an all-hands meeting. Monthly, you will do the financial review. On a weekly basis, you will conduct leadership team meetings and one-on-one meetings with your key managers. And finally, daily, you have a stand-up meeting.

Figure 9-2, The Perfect Business Meeting Rhythm.

The two key tools that support this rhythm are the *task logs* that prevent commitments from being forgotten and track them until they're completed and the *dashboard* that communicates all the necessary metrics to monitor performance, just like the dashboard of your car.

The strategic planning day. The strategic planning day is an offsite retreat that usually lasts about a day. During this time, you will review the past, examine the present situation, and then set the initiatives for the year ahead. Also, the leadership will gather to think and plan strategically.

The agenda for the day, tuned to the entrepreneurial sized business, is focused on fast planning. It goes as follows:

1. Review your accomplishments for the prior year.
2. Identify the challenges that cropped up.
3. Identify the lessons learned from those challenges.
4. Review your financials.
5. Review your progress on last year's initiatives.
6. Review the business plan for the year ahead.
7. Conduct an analysis of where you stand currently, including a summary of your strengths, weaknesses, opportunities, threats, and what is going on in the environment around you from the standpoint of changes in regulation, labor dynamics, supplier dynamics, and a competitive analysis to check in with what the competitors are doing and see how you match up against them.
8. Identify the initiatives for the year that flow out of the opportunities and threats.
9. Condense the initiatives and prioritize the few most important ones that will change the business.
10. Clarify those initiatives and assign ownership of them to the various team members.

These steps set up the year and establish the goals not just for operating the business but for improving it as well. The first time we went through these steps with Safety Service, Steve was surprised by how much the team contributed to the plan, and he regained his motivation to grow. At the same time, he saw that there was a conflict in his leadership team—some were interested in making changes while others wanted to go backward. Although bringing this conflict out into the open was unpleasant, it forced Steve to make some personnel decisions that enabled the company to move forward.

The quarterly planning session. The quarterly planning session usually lasts half a day. (Steve is able to run it in less than three hours with his team now that they are used to the format.) It can be a condensed version of the strategic planning day, and it is focused on looking ahead and setting goals for a 13-week timeframe.

In this session, you will be settling on the few most important projects that you are going to accomplish over the coming quarter. The format is as follows:

1. Review your accomplishments for the quarter.
2. Identify the challenges that cropped up.
3. Identify the lessons learned from those challenges.
4. Conduct a financial and operating review (including a view of the sales forecast versus the plan).
5. Review your progress on last quarter's projects.
6. Identify the projects you want to accomplish over the upcoming quarter by referring back to the strategic planning initiatives you chose. Make sure the projects are in harmony with your long-term goals.
7. Prioritize the few most important projects.
8. Clarify the projects by making them SMART (specific, measurable, achievable, result-oriented, and time-based) and assign ownership of them to the various players.

The all-hands meeting. The other quarterly interval meeting is the all-hands meeting. In this meeting, you bring together the whole team and update them on the results of the quarterly planning work that you just completed. You will also support the cultural rituals that we discussed in the prior chapter around recognition, gratitude, and keeping the team informed about what the future holds, the vision, and the challenges ahead.

The financial review. To match the accounting cycle, which is monthly, you will do the financial review once a month. You can add it to the weekly leadership team meeting once a month. Here you will review your financials and your key operating data. As you have already communicated much of the information via the dashboard you will be using weekly and daily, this will be a quick edition that focuses on the P&L balance sheet and statement of cash flows.

The weekly leadership team meeting. This is the meeting that ensures accountability and focus. The purpose of the meeting is to keep the projects moving forward and solve problems that crop up week to week. It's designed to be 90 minutes, but you can adapt it to be 60 or 75 minutes, depending on your particular needs. What is important is that you never allow it to exceed the timeframe you have established. Set an exact time every week, at the same time and with the same players every week, and make it happen regardless of anyone's absence, even the owner's. If the owner can't participate, find a substitute to run the meeting. The person best equipped to run the meeting is the person who is best at enforcing the timeframes and keeping the focus during the discussion and keeping it moving (which may not necessarily be the owner!). Designate a scribe for the meeting who can keep track of the conversation and the commitments made in the meeting. The dashboard you will be using will be prepared in advance. You will have the agenda up on a computer so you can update it live and have it ready for distribution at the end. It will serve as a record of any commitments that are made. This is where Steve and his team started to see real progress on their priorities. As they were in agreement on what they should be doing and were all reporting in on their progress every week, little by little, they accomplished the small steps that led to the big goals getting checked off the list. Using the task log in the meeting is the key to always keeping track of who will do what based on what they have said. It will also gain commitment and agreement from all the players to which they will be held accountable.

The agenda of the weekly leadership team meeting is as follows:

1. (Five minutes.) Each participant around the table shares their greatest accomplishment from the last week.
2. (Ten minutes.) Dashboard review: Each owner of the numbers reports in on the results.
   a. Identify any action for the task log or discussion required for the discussion list.
   b. If a problem is identified, put it on the list for discussion later in the meeting. This is not the segment for long discussions or problem solving.
3. (Five minutes.) Sixty-second project status report: The owner of each project identified in the quarterly planning reports in on their progress in 60 seconds or less.
   a. Keep the focus on steady progress week to week, reporting on any milestones. This will prevent losing focus on the project and discovering at the end of the quarter that nothing was accomplished.
   b. Identify any action for the task log or discussion required for the discussion list. Again, this not the venue for problem solving.
4. (Ten minutes.) Task log update: Go through the commitments that people make in these meetings that they are expected to accomplish within one week. Unlike your personal task management system, this system is for tracking all of the task delegation that happens in the team. It will indicate who made the commitment and what they committed to do, and it has the preset timeframe that the task will be accomplished within a week, before the next meeting.
   a. The scribe of the meeting edits it live. If a task is done, delete it from the list. If it's not done, keep it on the list so that it reappears next week and continues to reappear until it's completed. That way, it's never lost.

    b.   Be clear and specific about the goals. Have only one owner per goal to clarify accountability.

    c.   Distribute it within minutes. It will serve as the agenda for next week.

5. (Fifty-five minutes.) Problem solving: Prioritize, solve, and document one matter from your discussion list at a time.

    a.   Choose the most important problem and focus on that first. Don't just start with the first one on the list or the easiest one, which is the natural temptation. You won't have time for everything on the list, and that is okay. Focus on what is most important, and drive it to conclusion.

    b.   During the discussion period, stay on track and avoid going down rabbit holes. The person who is running the meeting has to be able to enforce the discussion, stay on topic, and speak up when it wanders off topic.

    c.   Update the task log to document the decisions and record who needs to communicate what to whom, depending on the solutions. This is the key part of the process that builds in accountability from week to week.

6. (Five minutes.) Each participant around the table has an opportunity to say a few last words. This is not an opportunity to reopen any discussions.

At the conclusion, distribute the updated agenda to everyone who was at the meeting. It will reappear as the agenda next week so you keep track of everything.

One-on-one meetings. The other key meetings that happen on a weekly interval are the one-on-one meetings. This is where you meet with your key direct reports, and it is the fastest way to improve their performance. The meetings are for them and you both. It's an opportunity for them to solve their problems with your help and learn, and it's an opportunity for you to develop them as leaders and managers. It's also an opportunity for you to keep informed of what is going on and stay in front of problems. The timeframe is usually 20 to 30 minutes but no longer. The agenda is very simple. It goes as follows:

1. (Five minutes.) Review their particular metrics.
2. (Five minutes.) Look at their progress on the projects they own through the quarter.
3. Turn it over to them. Let them air their issues and seek your help.

They should come prepared with their questions and challenges so that you can help them remove the obstacles, teach them, challenge, encourage, or support them as appropriate, and help them solve their problems. What you don't want to do, though, is do their work for them or allow them to put their monkey on your back. Just like the weekly leadership team meeting, this is at a set time every week.

Stand-up meetings. On the daily interval, you will conduct stand-up meetings, either at the departmental level or at the whole company level, depending on your size. These meetings happen at a set time and are always mandatory. Of all of the execution systems they implemented at Safety Service, it was the stand-up meetings that were met with the most resistance from the project manager team. Their reluctance seemed logical on its face: Why take the time when they all sit in the same room with each other all day long? A few months of sticking to the stand-up meetings showed them that, in spite of their close physical quarters, they weren't getting the focus, situational awareness, and control of their crews the old way. The daily meetings are now an indispensable habit for them.

The agenda of the daily stand-up meetings is as follows:

1. Review the metrics.
2. Ask the following questions around the table:
   a. What got done yesterday?
   b. What will happen today?
   c. Where are you stuck?

The meetings serve as daily touch points to maintain the pace and direction of your work. The purpose of them is a short identification of any challenges. As they last only 15 minutes, and not a minute more, there is no time to solve problems. If any are identified, they can be handled outside of the meetings afterward between the involved players so as not to waste anyone else's time.

The two tools that support this are the task management system we already discussed and the dashboard. The dashboard should be formatted to include the owner of all metrics. It should communicate the trend in the metric and provide some context in the form of a goal, a standard that you measure against, or numbers from a prior period or last year, or all of these to help understand the meaning behind the numbers. It usually takes the form of an excel spreadsheet that is updated weekly or a shared document that is stored in the cloud such as Google Sheets. The best way to communicate this kind of numerical information is graphically.

You should have neither too many nor too few metrics to observe. Ten is about right. Choose the ones that are most important for your situation. The best thing to do is to follow the key accountabilities of the management team for guidelines for what should be on the dashboard. Think of it as the tool you would use if you were sitting on the beach on vacation and wanted to check how the business was doing every day without talking to anybody. Those are the metrics you want to have on the dashboard. They should be predictive and actionable. Examples from sales and marketing are leads, proposals and their associated conversion rates, the number of new customers, the number of repeat customers, and the average order size. Examples from operations might be the backlog level and the units or dollars delivered, quality, on-time delivery, unplanned overtime, and customer satisfaction indexing. Financial examples are revenue, collection time, liquidity ratios, and gross margins like the ones we discussed in Chapter 8: Finance.

In this system, you have it all. You have the right frequency to maintain focus, and you have the tools to keep track of tasks on the right things. It enables you to monitor progress and correct course throughout the quarter to make sure you accomplish your big priorities, and that allows you to control the action to keep the progress moving.

CHAPTER 10

Operations

In the Introduction, I mentioned the story of Bill, a co-owner of VCI Mobility, a company in the business of converting vans and light commercial vehicles for accessibility for both the private and commercial markets in greater Philadelphia. In 2010, Bill and his business partner, Jack, were in a difficult situation. Over the prior 10 years, sales had gradually grown, but operationally, things were out of control. As Bill put it, "From 2001 to 2007, we probably went through four or five controllers. It was a mess. We didn't have any good internal systems. We had the good fortune of hiring some people who happened to be personally organized and who created their own systems. Those were all just sort of personal systems that existed within the business." Even though they were growing, there were many challenges. The morale of the team was up and down, and although they were working hard and long hours, they were far behind on deliveries.

Well aware that something had to change, Bill and his partner kept trying different things to turn around the situation. Like many other business owners who find themselves in this situation, they prioritized increasing sales in the belief that if they had enough revenue coming in, they could figure out everything else. But everything else proved to be elusive, and increasing sales was like pouring gasoline on a burning fire. They saw the crises multiply faster than the sales went up.

In the operation of your business, the activities that create value for your customers, you might be experiencing bottlenecks, mistakes in productions, or similar to what Bill and Jack did, people who know how to do things but perform in accordance with their mood or ability to remember all the steps of what they do. In that situation, it's easy to think you're stuck. You feel like you can't give up because so much depends on continuing the business, such as the jobs you support, the money you need, and all the other obligations of ownership. On the other hand, you don't think you can grow because you don't believe that the business can handle more volume. You're afraid that the wheels will come off. So you're trapped. You wish the work were done faster, with more visibility into the working process. You wish it were done more consistently, which would lead to better quality, fewer customer issues, and perhaps timely delivery. Overall, you want to move faster, but with less effort. You want to do more with less, which is leverage.

FROM TRIBAL TO INSTITUTIONAL

You want to move from a tribal method of keeping and communicating the knowledge necessary to run the business to an institutional method. With a tribal method, all the knowledge required to operate the business is fungible because it's locked up in everyone's mind. It can only be passed down by word of mouth. And that only happens if you're lucky. Oftentimes, the knowledge leaves with the key players. If they leave before their replacements have been hired, the replacements are left to figure things out on their own. When you go from word of mouth to words on paper and make your method institutional, you make the knowledge, the know-how, live in the business instead of in any one particular person's mind. When this method is implemented properly, anyone can understand, step by step, how to create value for your customer. Then they can make better decisions, move more quickly, and learn the job faster. Consistency for all the routine aspects of your operations will increase. Accountability will improve because of the transparency it brings. It will help with cost control and give visibility into problems or potential problems before they happen. And it will make managing the organization and changing it when necessary a lot easier.

When you go through this transformation, you open a can of worms. It's a good thing, though, because when you dig in, you will uncover all kinds of issues, gaps, and weaknesses that you probably never knew existed. Or maybe you did know, but you were living in a state of denial about them. This is typical. Although these issues may make it tough going at times, finding and resolving the ones that stand in the way of productivity is the path to success.

For the transition to be successful, you have to follow the rule of simplicity—make things as simple as possible but not any more than that. Set up the system so anyone new can come in and use it to learn how to do their job. It has to be usable. If it's not usable, it won't be followed. It's important to involve the team in the creation of these.

Most important is your mindset. Maybe you have been down this road before and failed because you didn't see the value in doing it and therefore you or your team didn't commit the time needed to get the work done. Or perhaps office politics got in the way. Maybe you were working on it in a group, and the loudest voice in the room took over, and no one stopped it, so it distorted the outcome. Or it could be that things were very bad, but the environment was such that no one wanted to speak up about it because they were ashamed of it or worried that they might lose face, so the problem never surfaced and got resolved. Or perhaps you didn't have the patience to deal with all the details that came with opening the can of worms, so you just gave up. You didn't have the grit to get through it.

The lessons here are first to get in the mindset by deciding that this is important and taking action to get momentum (you can go back to Chapter 3 for more specific details on how to do that). Next, be aware of the politics. You need everyone's help and participation, so you must balance the voices in the room. Also, you will have to dig deep and keep on digging. It's a big job. Prioritize it carefully so you can take small steps to get success quickly and maintain your focus throughout the process.

THE PERFECT BUSINESS SYSTEM

The Perfect Business System is comprised of five key elements.

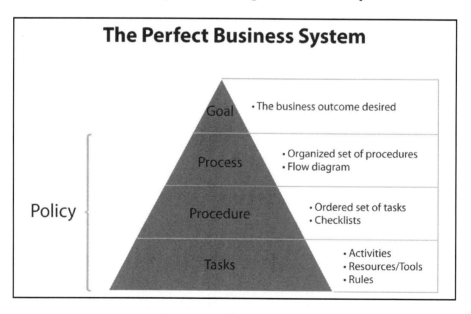

Figure 10-1, The Perfect Business.

It starts at the basic *task* level. At this level are the activities that everyone does, the resources or tools they need to do the job, and whatever rules they need to follow. The tasks assemble into an ordered list, which is a *procedure*. It is composed of all the tasks required to do a discrete step. They are most commonly expressed through checklists, which are the ordered sets of tasks. The procedures as a collection comprise the *process*, which can be thought of as a higher-level collection of procedures. It is usually expressed in a flow diagram that involves all the players and the workflow. All of this is driven by a particular *goal*—a desired outcome that you are trying to achieve. All of it is governed by the company's policies, the rules by which you have to do business.

So how do you create The Perfect Business System? You use the 4-Step System Building Process introduced earlier. The four steps of the process are: *prioritize, analyze, optimize,* and *institutionalize.*

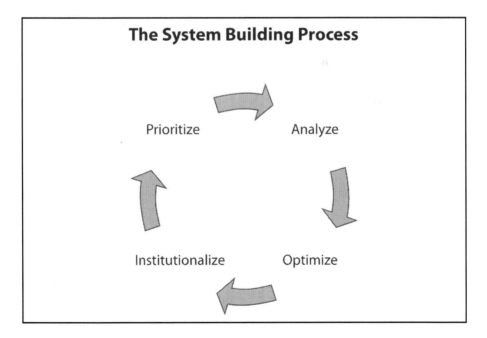

Figure 10-2, The System Building Process.

Let's dig a little deeper into each of those steps and see how they can apply in the systematization of your operation.

Prioritize. The first step in systemizing your operation is to list the key processes, the core functions, in your business. When you have done that, you want to triage what presents the biggest cost and risk in terms of the money or energy it wastes, the time it takes, the number of mistakes it creates, and the customer aggravation it causes, and focus on that. Work on the worst first. At VCI, Bill and Jack assessed the business overall to identify their key processes. They listed all the processes on a board, and then we looked for where the greatest pain was coming from. We discovered that their sales process of converting someone's decision to purchase and their choice in product attributes into the delivery of the correct product in the right timeframe was quite complex. There were many parties involved in the process. The controller was involved with reporting, compensation tracking, job costing, and bookkeeping. The administration team had to deal with all the contracts and the communication with the various government agencies that were often involved. The manufacturing team needed to do their scheduling and resource planning. Outside vendors needed to be contacted for ordering purposes, and then there were other outsiders like lenders, insurers, and government agencies that had to be involved as well. It was a complete mess. The information that was communicated to the different parties was late, missing, or wrong, and that caused delays and missed budgets for sales, late deliveries, upset customers, and just general mayhem. Working with the sales process wouldn't cost anything other than energy and focus on solving the problem, but it could have a huge impact, so we began by doing that.

Analyze. After identifying which process to work on first, you analyze it and get an understanding of how it is done now by breaking down its existing state. In the course of doing so, you will identify bottlenecks, weaknesses, and risks, but you will also get a baseline of from where you start. First, you want to define or re-confirm the goal you are trying to accomplish to make sure that you are fundamentally working on the right purpose. Write a rough draft of the process using the key steps. Then dig deeper into the spaces in between those steps to fill in the details, because that's where the opportunities will be to eliminate the friction in the workflow. This is a top-down exercise. At VCI, we drew out the existing system on the wall of their conference room with labeled sticky notes. We moved around and organized the notes until we got a semblance of how the process was at the time. Then we documented it on an Excel spreadsheet. That is how we got the baseline. In the course of doing so, we identified many gaps and weaknesses.

Optimize. When you have analyzed the process, you can optimize it. You begin by gathering all the stakeholders who know how to do the work. Design the process level, including all the steps in the right order, branches where decisions are required, and any other procedures that might come into play. Then you have to get clear on who is in charge of each procedure and the process as a whole. You also have to get clear on whether the customers for the process are internal or external. When you have done that, you can build the flow diagram.

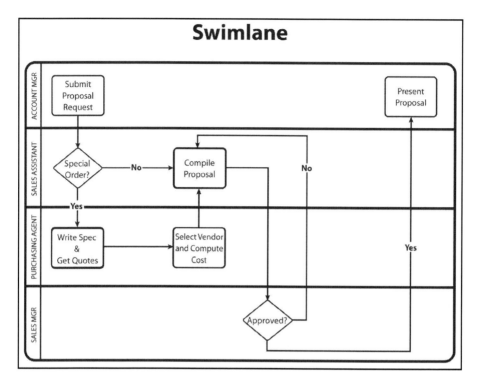

Figure 10-3, Swimlane diagram.

As these processes and procedures are dynamic and will frequently be updated, you need to come up with a scheme for revision control—a tool to track that you are working on the most current ones.

After designing the process, the next step is to design the tasks, the individual discrete steps, which are comprised of the individual activity. Clarify who will do that activity. It can only be one person. Although that may sound obvious, multiple people often take responsibility for the same activities unless the responsibility is clarified, and that generates a lot of confusion. Next, you will identify the vehicles for moving around information that are needed for the particular task. These are artifacts like checklists, templates, scripts, reports, spreadsheets, databases, forms, or software that you will use. You will also identify the time constraints—expected duration of the task and any deadlines and triggers. In addition, you will identify any policies that govern the activities. An example of a policy that you have to abide by could be that you won't start production without payment from the customer. This policy wouldn't necessarily appear in every process you write, but it governs what you do nevertheless, so you need to identify it and document it.

When you have designed the tasks, you need to make sure they work before you commit to them fully, so you need to implement them on a test basis and adjust them as needed. The first things we did when we gathered the team at VCI were to get clear on the goal and make sure that everyone understood the *why* behind the work we were about to undertake. We gathered the small groups of people and let everyone have their say about their part of the process. Then we put all the paperwork on the table, found all the problems, and started working on all the solutions. We uncovered many problems that were causing delays, so we had to do a lot of reorganization. It took a series of meetings to accomplish all this in small bites.

Institutionalize. Finally, you will institutionalize the process. The first step here is to train and educate the team. Changing the process often results in changing the way you do business, so people will need to get out of their old habits and into new ones. That will require that you give them not only instruction on the new steps but also education on why you are implementing the changes and some sense of purpose about what they are accomplishing.

Next, you have to find a way to manage the system artifacts, the diagrams, and all the documents of the procedures, including the scripts, templates, etc., that go along with the system. You can accomplish that in a file system, either on the premises or in the cloud. The simplest way would be to create an Excel table that includes an outline of the work along with hyperlinks to the various Word documents and templates you use. You could take a similar approach using Google Docs. There is also a wide range of specialized software available that is both on the premises and cloud-based that does this, so choose the one that is best suited for your organization.

Lastly, select key performance indicators that will enable you to manage the process via periodic reports. The key performance indicators are tools you use to know if things are working or not. Examples of KPIs in operations are utilization rates. These measure the efficiency with which you use the assets and the resources to do the work. One utilization rate is the billable ratio, which is hours billed divided by total hours worked. If someone spent 30 of the 40 hours they worked one week on client projects, their billable ratio would be 30 divided by 40, or 75%. Another utilization rate is the capacity utilization rate, which is hours used divided by hours available in a given time period. If a machine ran for five out of eight hours in a shift, its production capacity utilization rate is five divided by eight or 63%. Another example of a KPI in operation is order fulfillment cycle time. This measures the time from when an order is placed until it's fulfilled. It is measured and averaged in days or hours, depending on your business, in a given period. You can also use the DIFOT rate, which is an acronym for "delivery in full, on time." That is the number of successful deliveries divided by total deliveries in a given period, for example, a week or a month. A successful delivery is counted as such if it's both done in full and made on time. For example, if you successfully delivered 90 out of 95 attempts in a month, your DIFOT rate is 90 divided by 95 or 95%. For a more comprehensive list of KPIs, please visit www.johnsheridan.com.

When you have these numbers, it's useful to express them in a way that shows their trend and frequency. Although your KPI results may be compared to a goal or benchmark to judge your performance, you need to understand the trend to put it in context and be able to act on it. Here is an example of information expressed in both a table and a chart.

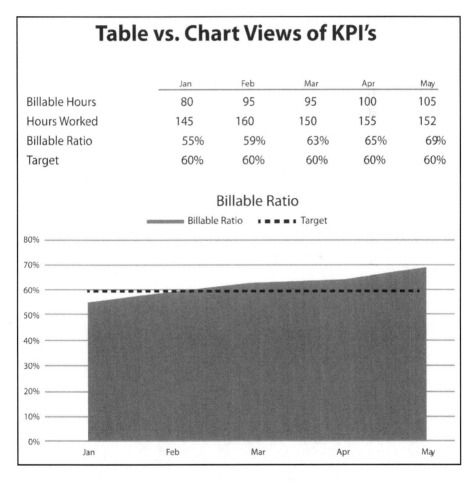

Figure 10-4, Table vs. Chart View of KPI's.

Here is an example of information in three different formats to illustrate the difference between the numbers presented in a simple table versus the same set of numbers expressed in a bar chart, which is a typically used approach, and a cumulative graph, which communicates the overall effect over time in a much more intuitive way. The scorecard displays the information in a table format.

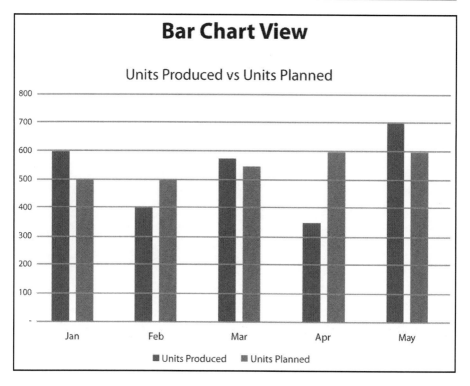

Scorecard View

	Jan	Feb	Mar	Apr	May
Units Produced	600	400	575	350	700
Units Planned	500	500	550	600	600
Cumulative Production	600	1,000	1,575	1,925	2,625
Cumulative Plan	500	1,000	1,550	2,150	2,750

Bar Chart View

Units Produced vs Units Planned

■ Units Produced ■ Units Planned

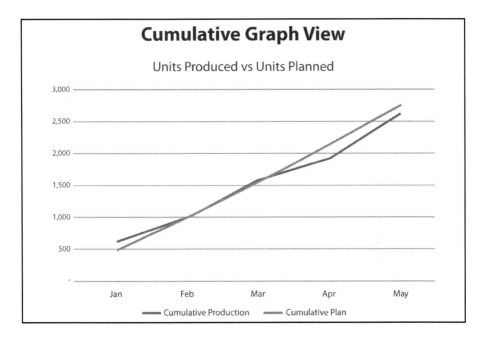

Figure 10-5, Figure 10-6 and Figure 10-7, the Scorecard, Bar Chart and Cumulative Graph View of Production Units respectively.

While working on VCI, we discovered that by using the reports, we could find more gaps. When the numbers didn't look right, there was a root cause we had to understand. We kept working at it until the team was self-sufficient in diagnosing their problems. Eventually, it got to the point where and Bill and Jack could manage the business with just a few meetings a week. The systems and the team handled the rest of it. People now had the information and resources they needed and were meeting on their own initiative to improve their systems. It was a remarkable transformation.

CHECKLISTS

When developing your procedures, you will discover that checklists are the most common type of resource used to operate your systems. Here are a few of the best practices to use when developing your checklists to make them effective (for more, see Atul Gawande's *The Checklist Manifesto):*

- Name it with words that are clear and include the objective of the checklist itself.
- Involve the team in its creation. This is not just a top-down exercise; it is a top-down and bottom-up exercise.
- Use seventh-grade-reading-level language. Keep it simple. A great way to test the language is to read the list aloud before publishing it.
- Use a clear format with no crowding or too much information.
- Fit it on one page. Avoid using colors if you can. Use a sans serif font, and never use all caps.
- Test it and update it.
- Make it easy to use and build in steps that catch the common mistakes before they happen to prevent them from becoming huge problems.

Technology is making all of this work easier than ever, and more effectively too. There are several software packages that you can use to document workflows that are simple to use and very affordable. Video is becoming the training tool of choice. You can record your screen to demonstrate a procedure and include your narration to document it and then use it as a training tool for new team members. One task at a time, you can build a library of videos that can teach anyone to operate your business.

The opportunity to systemize your business is everywhere. You just have to dig to bring all the problems to the surface. Then you can organize the systems and update them in a way that makes your business run smoothly.

CHAPTER 11

Lead Generation

If you ask any entrepreneur what they need most to grow their business, the first answer you will hear is always, "More leads." Although that is not always true, it's the one thing that is on everyone's mind. And that is understandable because they are used to having an insufficient number of leads or a lot of unqualified leads that they have to sift through to find qualified ones. To generate leads, they tend to bounce around from strategy to strategy, which leads to inconsistency, and frankly, they don't know where their new business is going to come from next. If they systemize lead generation correctly, however, they can get a steady stream of leads that are warmed up and qualified for them from different sources. They can design the system in such a way that they can be confident they will have the lead flow they want and drive the number of leads they need based on the budget they have to spend.

Before we go into the system, let's examine the changes that are happening in the world that have had an impact on how marketing is done. Strategically speaking, the world has changed largely because of the internet. Now that information is available everywhere, buyers, both consumers and business buyers, are searching and collecting information well before they engage with a seller. As a result, they are much more informed, and their buying process has changed dramatically. Entrepreneurs have had to adapt to that change. Tactically speaking, there is now an abundance of inexpensive and effective tools available, including automation of customer relationship management (CRM) and communication, analysis of the effectiveness of online advertising, and extremely targetable advertising on social media sites. We can see the change in how advertisers are allocating their advertising budgets. Digital spending has now surpassed television spending. One out of every four advertising dollars is now spent on digital, and we are crossing the $100-billion-per-year ad spend threshold in digital in the United States.

While these factors have dramatically affected the way we do marketing, the world is still the same in many ways. It's still critical to master the fundamentals, that is, we have to be crystal clear on who our target is, find a way to get our message in front of that target, and make our message carry with it a value proposition that resonates with them. In other words, strategy comes first. Then we have to develop ways to get the target to do something, whether that is to call for an appointment, opt into a list or buy something directly. Whatever actions they are, we need to design and test them so that they are predictable.

Digital technology tends to distract owners. It gets all their attention because it's bright, shiny, and new, and it's fun to learn about it and experiment with it. It isn't the whole picture, though. To stand out in the flood of information that targets your prospects, you must be unique, and you have to be in front of them frequently and consistently. That won't happen without a system.

An ad hoc approach of testing the latest fad and then dropping it after a month or two because it doesn't work will work against you. Rather than keeping trying many different approaches and hoping to stumble upon a home run, you should develop one or two strategies intensively and refine them before jumping from idea to idea.

Another challenge is that there is no one formula or mix of channels or tactics that will work. You have to discover it. You have to design it and build it and test it while minimizing the expense along the way until you find a recipe that works. Then you can scale it up.

CREATING A SYSTEMIZED APPROACH TO LEAD GENERATION

To create a systemized approach to lead generation, you need to undergo three shifts in your thinking. First, you have to let go of guesswork—using hunches, guesses, or gut-feel as a method to choose lead generation strategies. Instead of using gut-feel to understand where your leads and new customers come from, shift to using *measurement* to get a handle on what it costs to acquire new customers, where they are coming from, what is working, what is not working, and the return on the investment that you are making to acquire them. Once you have that baseline of measurements, you can move from measurement to *optimization*. That means using all the information you have, analyzing it, stopping or fixing the inefficient channels and tactics, and reallocating your investment to the high-performing ones. Next, you want to improve the high-performing channels so you can lower the cost of acquiring new customers. Then you want to repeat that process for each of your channels until you have an appropriate set of strategies that you can count on to produce leads for every dollar you spend. The third shift you need to make is to go from optimization to a *budget-*

driven marketing investment. When you have your costs and ROI dialed in, you can predict how many leads will result from any given level of investment you make. You can then reverse engineer your business plan to compute your marketing budget.

MAKING THE THREE SHIFTS

Here's how Securitas, an information security consultancy, was able to drive up sales by taking a measuring stick to their lead generation efforts and tweaking their approach to grow a steady flow of qualified prospects for their security assessment service engagements. Through analysis of their history, we learned the following statistics: For every sale they closed, they had produced four written proposals, so their proposal to sale conversion rate was 25%. To get to the opportunity to present their proposal, their sales team would conduct two sales appointments for a conversion rate of 50%. Their sales appointments resulted from leads they received from weekly educational webinars they produced, and one out of every 10 webinar attendees liked what they learned and requested a sales appointment. So their webinar attendee to sales conversion rate was 10%. After analyzing their spending, we determined that it cost them $25 for every attendee on the webinars. Knowing that information, we were able to reverse engineer and design a budget to drive better performance.

Securitas' owner Joe created a business plan that assumed he could acquire two new customers per week, which we know from our analysis would require two divided by 0.25 or eight written proposals. To get those eight proposals, they had to have 16 sales appointments, and to get 16 sales appointments from the webinars at a 10% conversion rate, they needed to have 160 webinar attendees. If they needed 160 attendees, and they spent $25 per attendee, they needed to make the product of $4,000 in marketing investment per week to achieve the plan.

Joe figured that if he wanted to acquire three new customers instead, he could just change the numbers. Three new customers divided by 0.25 would require 12 proposals. Twelve proposals divided by 50% would require 25 appointments. Those appointments divided by 10% would require 250 webinar attendees. At $25 per attendee, it would drive a $6,250 marketing investment. The only problem was that it didn't work. We had to dig a little deeper to find out what was happening.

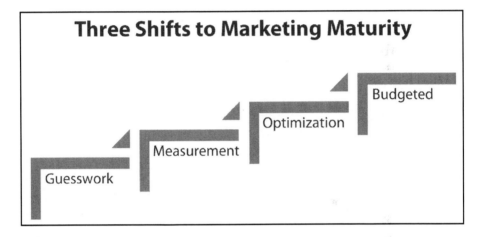

Figure 11-1, Three Shifts to Marketing Maturity model.

Systemizing the marketing requires evidence-based decision making, which means we need to understand the evidence first, so we wanted to begin with measuring all the existing information we had. In addition to counting how many leads were coming in, we looked at which channels they came from, whether they came from an online advertising campaign, an email campaign, direct mail, customer referral, external referral, etc. To find that out, we asked the customers and tracked their answers with the CRM system. Although we won't always know exactly which source, we can get it right about 80% of the time with reasonable confidence.

Then we segregated their total marketing investment into each channel and calculated how much they were spending on email, direct mail, pay-per-click (PPC), *search engine optimization* (SEO), and additional advertising.

The next step was to compute the three key metrics that would explain the effectiveness of the marketing. Those were the cost per lead (CPL), the cost per acquisition of a new customer (CPA), and the marketing return on investment (MROI). We analyzed these metrics for each of the various channels they used to drive attendees to their webinar. Here is what we learned after a month of testing:

Channel	Spend	Leads (Webinar Attendess	Cost Per Lead	New Customers	Cost per Adquisition
PPC	$18,240	847	$22	1	$18,240
SEO	$ 6,000	112	$54	7	$ 857
Email	$ 800	42	$20	0	
Total	$25,080	997	$25	8	$ 3,135

Figure 11-2, Securitas Customer Acquisition Cost by Channel Analysis.

It turned out that the leads that came from PPC sources weren't converting in spite of the increased spend. Although SEO had the highest cost per lead, it was the clear winner based on cost per acquisition. The next move was clear: fix the PPC campaign, reallocate budget to SEO, or both. They did both. SEO continues to have the lowest cost per acquisition because it attracts more qualified prospects to them.

The MROI is calculated by computing the new gross margin for every new customer acquired, subtracting the marketing cost it took to acquire them, and then dividing that result by the total marketing investment it took to get them. In the case of Securitas, let's suppose that each of the eight new sales they win was a $20,000 project that had a 40% gross margin. Then the new gross margin they brought in would be eight projects multiplied by $20,000, which would result in $160,000 in revenue, multiplied by 40%, which would yield a new gross margin of $64,000. Here's the MROI calculation broken down for PPC vs. SEO:

	PPC	SEO	Total
Revenue	$20,000	$140,000	$160,000
40% Gross Margin	$ 8,000	$ 56,000	$ 64,000
Acquisition Cost	$18,240	$ 6,000	$ 24,240
Net Gross Margin	$10,240	$ 50,000	$ 39,760
MROI	- 56%	833%	164%

Figure 11-3, Securitas MROI Analysis

We see that the marketing investment in PPC actually caused a loss. The SEO channel, on the other hand, produced 833% return or about $8 of new gross margin for every $1 invested. Although it's not always this dramatic, this shows how important it is to dig deep to understand exactly how you are acquiring new business through your lead generation system. Once you know that, you can start to make evidence-based decisions about which campaigns you are running that are working and which are not.

That leads us to the next step in making the three shifts, which is optimization. First, you need to weed out the ineffective campaigns based on the numbers we just calculated. Then you can choose one channel at a time and begin split testing by making small variations in the campaigns—changing in the headlines, copy, photography, artwork, or even list segmentation you use.

Next, you track the results carefully and compute the key metrics again. Keep weeding out the losers and retesting the winners over and over again as you drive down your cost per lead and your cost per acquisition. Then you can add initiatives one channel at a time by testing new things you aren't doing already while focusing on building your most important lead generation asset—your database of prospects.

It takes diligence and persistence to optimize lead generation, but when you begin to see the cost per acquisition drop, and you begin to have confidence in your marketing mix, it becomes like a game.

CHAPTER 12

Conversion

Although the process of converting leads into paying customers must be systematic in order to be predictable, usually it's not. In fact, most business owners don't even know their conversion rate because they don't measure it. Not knowing this basic information leads to a lot of the typical frustrations that come with ad hoc selling. Without visibility into each step of the process, it's difficult to diagnose what is off track when things go wrong. Also, when a sales rep leaves the company and takes their knowledge and relationships with them, sales will take a dip because there is nothing to fall back on to recover or to train the replacement. Likewise, when the existing team exhibits inconsistent performance, it's difficult to pinpoint exactly where they are going wrong, and that slows down not only the diagnosis but also the formulation of a remedy to get sales back on track. Chronic underperformance can cause the owner to think that they are stuck with a team that just can't or won't improve. In fact, the issues more often stem from problems in the process. That's good news because it's easier to fix the process than to replace the people.

What you want in a well-designed conversion system is predictability. Because the process depends more on the power of the systems than the strength of the sales rep, sales goals get achieved more consistently. When you have all these elements in place, you have a system that you can believe in that will get you results.

There are two main drivers of a successful conversion system: the quality of the people and the quality of the process.

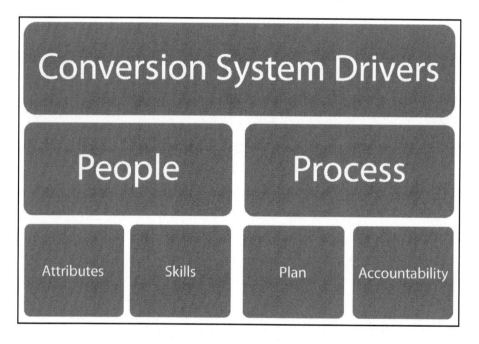

Figure 12-1, Conversion System Drivers.

Since we covered behavioral attributes and skills that play a big role in the success of conversion in Chapter 7, Performance Management, we will now focus on the other driver, which is the quality of the process. The process comes down to the plan for getting the sale and some accountability mechanism to make sure it happens the way you want it to happen.

FOUR KEY PRINCIPLES OF THE CONVERSION SYSTEM

There are four principles you want to design into your system: *written goals and a plan, leverage, visibility,* and *accountability.*

Written goals and a plan. First, you must have written goals and a plan. The goals should be specific, measurable, and realistic. These are easier to create than the plan, but it's the plan—the specific idea of how you will achieve the various activities necessary to get to the finish line—that will make those goals happen. You need to translate the annual plan into a quarterly, monthly, weekly, and daily action plan that the sales team can follow.

Leverage. Next, you need leverage. This means identifying and focusing your time and resources on two things: the right accounts and the right activities. The right accounts are the ones that are the correct size and opportunity as opposed to the smaller, less important ones. The right activities are those that will yield the results you want.

Visibility. You also need visibility into every part of the process. Breaking it down and measuring it will show you where the weak points are, which makes diagnosis and repair much easier. It will also make improvement much more specific and targeted so you can take small steps that will yield large results.

Accountability. In addition, you must incorporate some accountability into the process. It will help you manage the amount of sales activities required to produce the desired sales volume in your plan. It will also maintain focus on the high-leverage activities that we just discussed. Lastly, it ensures that the plans are executed over time so that you can enable course correction before it's too late.

SYSTEM FOR IMPROVING CONVERSION

Divide up your sales process. Before you can operate the conversion process, you need to build it, so let's start with dividing your sales process into basic stages that comprise your *funnel*. The funnel is usually divided into six or seven stages. Here is a typical breakdown:

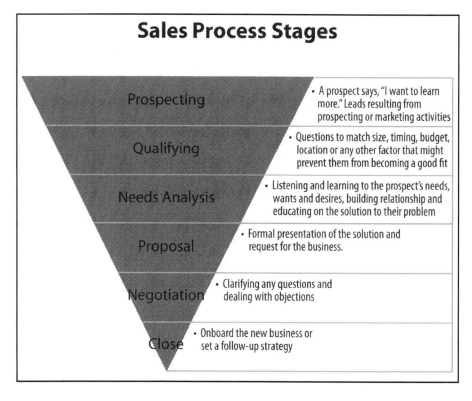

Figure 12-2, Sales Process Stages.

The first stage is prospecting. That is when a prospect says, "I want to learn more" in response to your marketing or outbound sales efforts like prospecting, networking, referrals, etc. From there, you move the prospect into the qualifying stage, which is where you ask questions to make sure that they are the correct size, their timing is right, they have the right budget, they are in the right place, or any other factor that might prevent them from being a good fit as a customer. You must get that information on the table right away to make sure you are spending your time with the right people. If the prospect is qualified, you move them into the needs-analysis stage. That is when you listen and learn about the prospect's needs, wants, and desires. You build a relationship with them and educate them on your solution to their problem. If the needs analysis leads to a chance of doing business, the next stage is to create a proposal. That is when you make a formal presentation of your solution and ask for the business. Often, at that point, you go into a stage of negotiation where you clarify any questions, deal with objections as they may come up, and perhaps make some revisions to your proposal. Finally, you want to close the business. If you are successful, you onboard the new business into the flow of operations. If you aren't, you set up a follow-up strategy because although you sometimes will lose business to a competitor, the prospect's need often changes or is canceled or delayed, and you want to stay in touch to get a chance for the opportunity in the future.

Measure your effectiveness and efficiency. When you have divided your sales process into basic stages, you can measure your effectiveness—your level of activity—at each stage. Here is a set of typical key performance indicators that would accompany each of the stages we just identified. These measure the effectiveness that is largely driven by volume.

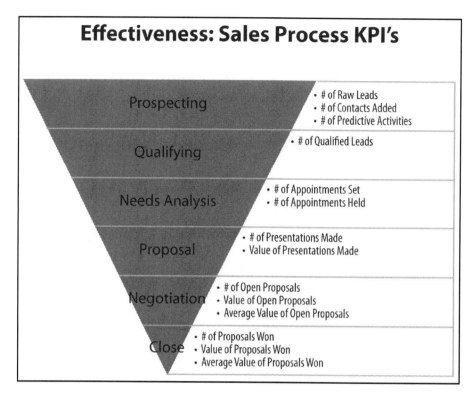

Figure 12-3, Effectiveness: Sales Process KPIs.

In the prospecting stage, you may look at the number of raw leads in any particular period, the number of contacts you added to your database, or perhaps the number of predictive activities, such as outbound sales calls, etc., that drive leads into your funnel. During the qualifying stage, you count the number of qualified leads. In the needs analysis stage, you count the number of appointments you can set in the given week, month, or day, and the number of appointments you have actually held. In the proposal stage, you count the number of presentations you have made and measure the total dollar value of those presentations. You can track the negotiation stage by monitoring the number of open proposals, that is, proposals that have been made but not yet won or lost. To get a sense of how the number changes from week to week and month to month, you can monitor the value of open proposals. Then you can measure the average value of each open proposal to make sure that you are talking to the right customers. Finally, in the closing stage, you can obviously count the number of proposals you have won. You can also measure the value of the proposals you have won or the average value of those proposals. Those are the key performance indicators you can use to measure the effectiveness of the sales process.

When you have measured the effectiveness of your process, you can do some calculations to measure the efficiency of it—how well you do it.

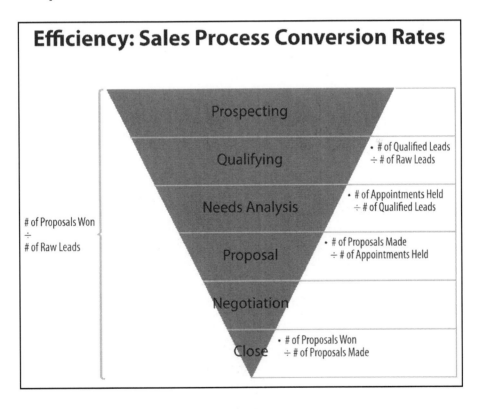

Figure 12-4, Efficiency: Sales Process Conversion Rates.

Here are some examples of how you can measure the efficiency in the same funnel. We will look at conversion rates. The qualifying ratio is the number of qualified leads you have divided by the number of raw leads you have. The needs analysis conversion ratio is the number of appointments you have held divided by the number of qualified leads you have. The proposal ratio is the number of proposals you have made divided by the number of appointments you have held. Finally, the close ratio is the number of proposals you have won divided by the number of proposals you made. By multiplying all these ratios, you get the overall conversion rate that measures the number of proposals won divided by the number of raw leads coming into the funnel.

Diagnose and improve. Now that you have a measure of not only the effectiveness but also the efficiency throughout the funnel, you can use it to diagnose and improve your sales process.

Here's an example of how that looks for Ace Packaging, a company in the business of selling boxes to industrial customers in their region of the country. They have marketing from their website, trade journals, email, and direct mail that support their sales, and they prospect for new customers as well. Here is a summary of their activity level for the month:

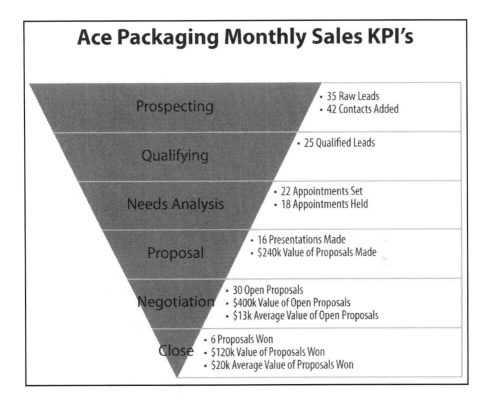

Figure 12-5, Ace Packaging Monthly Sales KPIs.

In prospecting, they generated 35 raw leads and added 42 contacts to their database. They qualified 25 of those raw leads as viable prospects. During the needs analysis stage, they set 22 appointments and held 18 appointments in the course of the month. They made 16 proposals for a total value of $240,000. Now they have 30 open proposals in negotiation. The aggregate value of the proposals is $400,000, and the average value per proposal is $13,000. They closed six of the 30 proposals this month for $120,000 of new business that they won at an average of $20,000 per new client.

We can now see into their pipeline and measure their conversion rates.

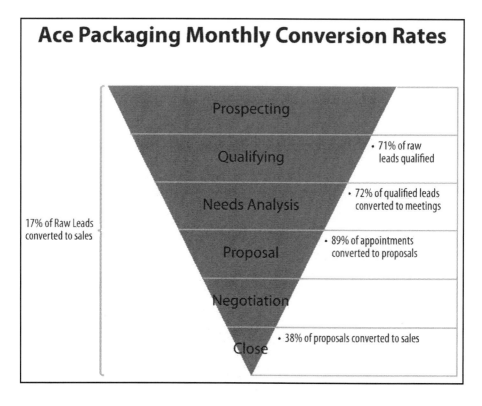

Ace Packaging Monthly Conversion Rates

Prospecting

Qualifying
- 71% of raw leads qualified

Needs Analysis
- 72% of qualified leads converted to meetings

17% of Raw Leads converted to sales

Proposal
- 89% of appointments converted to proposals

Negotiation

Close
- 38% of proposals converted to sales

Figure 12-6, Ace Packaging Monthly Conversion Rate.

With the numbers we have, we can calculate that of their raw leads, 71% qualified as good prospects. Of those qualified prospects, 72% lead to face-to-face meetings to conduct needs analysis. Those meetings resulted in appointments. Those appointments resulted in proposals 89% of the time, and they closed 38% of their proposals into sales. Overall, 17% of their raw leads converted to sales. These conversion rates can be used as a diagnostic tool. As they knew that they converted 17 out of every 100 raw leads into sales, and they wanted to increase sales without increasing their marketing investment to get more leads, they could look to their conversion rates and find ways to improve their efficiency with the leads they already had to get the lift they wanted.

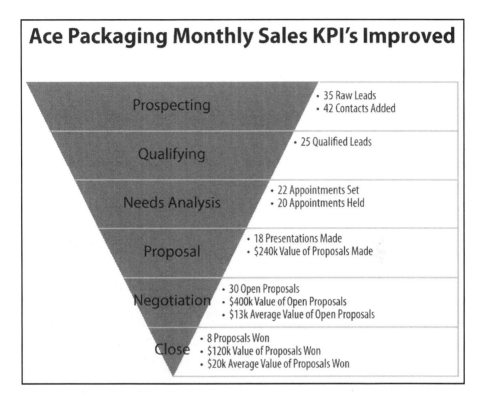

Figure 12-7, Ace Packaging Monthly Sales KPI's Improved.

To do that, they had to dig deeper into their process. First, they documented the individual steps in each stage of the funnel. Then they optimized them to get small increases in efficiency along the way. They focused on a few areas of their funnel to improve their results. First, they wanted to improve their rate for converting qualified leads into appointments. To optimize how they handled the discussions with their prospects at that stage, they built in new scripting to include the best practices gleaned from their historically top-performing sales reps. They also built in a step that called for an information package to be sent to the prospect immediately upon qualification in order to educate them about the business and build their trust. They wanted to improve their rate for converting appointments into proposals by sending out a written thank-you note after their face-to-face meetings with their prospects. They wanted to improve their closing ratio by handling their typical objections a little more effectively, so they consolidated the best practices around objection handling and built them into their scripting, and then they trained the team on how to deliver those scripts.

Here is the result of their efforts:

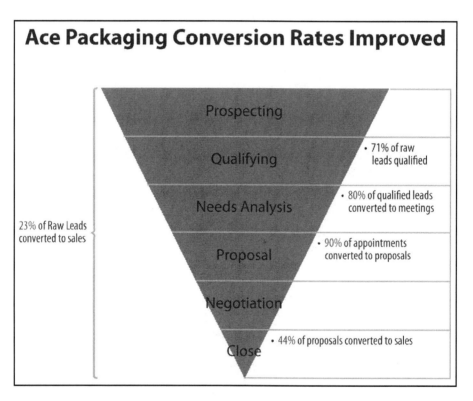

Figure 12-8, Ace Packaging Conversion Rates Improved.

As a result of their work, their needs analysis conversion ratio went up to 80%, their proposal ratio improved to 90%, and their close ratio improved to 44%. Their overall conversion rate became 23%. So by focusing on these three areas, documenting the process, optimizing each step, and training the team, they were able to improve their overall conversion rate by 35%.

Reverse engineer the process to reach your goals. Once you know your process, you can plan how you will achieve your goals. First, you have to set written goals, which is usually the least difficult part. Then, with the knowledge you have from your conversion rate analysis, you can reverse engineer your process into the specific activity levels you to need in order to achieve those goals. That will result in a realistic sales plan that you can execute.

Here's how it would apply to Ace Packaging. Let's say that they had a goal of bringing in $2.4 million from business with new clients in the upcoming year. Using their conversion rates working backward, to find the number of customers they would need to achieve that goal, they would divide the goal of $2.4 million by their average sale of $20,000, which would show that they needed 120 new customers. To identify the number of proposals they needed to make to generate 120 new customers, they divided 120 by their closing ratio of 44%. That showed them that they needed to make 273 proposals to generate the number of new customers they wanted. To know how many appointments they needed to set to get that number of proposals, they divided 273 by their 90% proposal ratio, which determined that they needed 303 appointments. The number of qualified leads they needed in order to generate that many appointments was 303 divided by their 80% appointment ratio—379 qualified leads. For that many qualified leads, they needed 379 divided by their 71% qualifying ratio—534 raw leads in order to fulfill this plan. To understand how many raw leads they needed to generate per week, they divided the total number of raw leads they needed for the year by the 50 weeks of selling time that they had in a year. It showed that they needed to generate 11 leads per week or about two per day. Now they could base their marketing and sales activities on a two-lead-per-day minimum standard to reach their goal.

Manage the sales activity. Once you have a plan, you want to make your team accountable to ensure that they uphold the standards. To do that, you can create a scorecard that reports on the sales plan activities for the team and the individuals on the team.

Sales activity scorecard example

Week of 10/16/17

	Inbound Leads	Outbound Leads	Total Leads	1st Meetings	New Proposals	Open Proposals	Won	Value
GOAL	2	4	6	3	3	12	3	$15,000
Mike	3	4	7	3	2	8	3	$18,000
Susan	2	5	7	2	2	10	3	$12,500
Jason	4	5	9	4	3	9	4	$22,000
Eric	3	3	6	2	2	12	4	$14,500
TEAM	12	17	29	11	9	39	14	$67,000

Figure 12-9, Sales Scorecard example.

Another way you can actively manage your sales activity is the pipeline management technique. It will probably be in the form of a report you can produce from the CRM that shows how many prospects there are and which prospects are in each stage of the funnel.

On a weekly basis, you can examine the report and monitor the progress of each account from one stage to the next.

On top of these steps, you can add an account-based selling system. Here is how you do that: For each of the reps, you create a list of the top 10 optimum accounts they want to break into.

They would be prioritized in order of size and opportunity. For example, if you have a large client who you are selling a little bit of business to, and you have a small share of their business, this client would be a high-priority prospect. Those would be the ones who you would want to focus your energy on consistently. When you have created the top-10 lists, you review the progress weekly as you examine the pipeline to make sure that you are making some positive steps toward breaking into those big accounts every week.

Now you are ready to train your people because you have a system that will support them. Although systemizing the conversion process takes a lot of energy and focus, the good news is it doesn't take very much, if any, cash outlay. It's a low-cash investment that can have a huge impact on your bottom line.

CHAPTER 13

Customer Retention

The most underappreciated strategy to grow a business systematically is first to prevent it from shrinking from loss of its existing customers. Owners neglect to give customer retention the attention it deserves because their strongest entrepreneurial drive is to focus their energy and attention on finding and closing the next new customer. That's where all the fun is. That's how they built the business.

A constant focus on the next new customer often leads to a lack of attention to keeping the hard-earned existing customer base. If you don't pay attention and build a system into your business to keep your customers, you will see unnecessarily high churn rates or customer attrition. You will overspend to find new customers to replace the ones you've lost. You will have a lower lifetime customer value (the profit they bring you over the entire period they are your customer), which reduces the return on investment of every marketing dollar you spend. As a result, growth can stall out because you lose customers at a faster rate than you can afford to spend to replace them. Worst of all, the market can shift before you can adapt because you weren't listening to your customers. Meanwhile, your competition is listening, and they might find a better way to serve your customers and push you aside in the process.

If you get your customer retention right, however, your retention rate and therefore your lifetime customer value will improve. In turn, your marketing investment will achieve a higher return. You will need to find fewer new customers, so your company will be less dependent on marketing and sales to survive, and you will achieve your planned sales a lot more easily. You will be closer to your customers, which translates to innovation to keep them satisfied and to keep your competitors at bay, not to mention more upselling, cross-selling, and referrals. In the end, you'll have a more predictable, stable, and easier-to-run business.

Losing a customer is an unforced error and a costly one. It costs lost referrals, which are the best leads you can get because they are presold, and it costs the money you have to spend to replace that customer. Usually, you have to spend six to nine times more to replace a customer than to keep an existing one. Also, although you will never hear why they left, they will tell their friends and associates about it. Think of the last time you were disappointed with a restaurant. When you have a bad experience, you usually won't bother to tell the owner or manager why; you just leave and never return. You might tell your friends why, though, and that word of mouth will have a negative impact on their reputation. A great way to quantify the cost of losing a customer is to think about this question: What if you had never lost a customer in the lifetime of your business? You can calculate the lost revenue from each customer you've ever lost, which is painful to do, but eye-opening.

Why do customers leave? Most often, they leave because they are dissatisfied with the service, not the price. It is a direct result of you or your team not paying them enough attention. Many business owners fear losing customers when thinking about things like increasing prices or making a change in the business, but few business owners take action to preserve their existing customer base. To understand how your customers feel and what they want so you can keep them, you need to build an active listening system into your business.

Consistency is important. Jan Carlzon, a former Chief Executive Officer of Scandinavian Airlines, once determined that in his business, there were 50,000 moments of truth every day. His idea of a moment of truth was every interaction between a customer and someone in his business. He figured that each one of those moments of truth was an opportunity for his business to make or break itself. There are likely thousands of moments of truth in your business as well. As you are only as good as your last interaction, consistency is key.

Not all customers are created equal. Here the Pareto Principle comes into play again. In this case, 20% of your customers likely provide 80% of your profit, sales, or both. The sad truth is that some of your customers need to go, while others, the small minority who provide most of the benefits, likely need more attention. Typically, it's the other way around; the customers who provide the least of the benefits receive most of the attention.

To help you avoid pouring water into a leaking bucket, let's dive into how you can keep the existing customers you worked so hard to find.

SATISFACTION DRIVERS

If keeping your customers is your goal, how do you do it? You need to dig deep to understand why customers stay. Retention is best predicted by customer satisfaction, which is not terribly surprising. But you need to understand more deeply what drives satisfaction. Customer satisfaction is a function of the customer's *perception of value* and their *expectation of value*. Here's a formula that explains how customers judge their level of satisfaction:

The Satisfaction Formula

$$S = PV - EV$$

Satisfaction = Perceived Value – Expected Value

Figure 13-1, The Satisfaction Formula.

Their level of satisfaction is the difference between what they perceived they got minus what they expected to get. So it's not just the perception of value that drives the satisfaction level; the expectation of value influences it as well. For that reason, it's important to understand the perception as it relates to what they expected that they would get. For example, if you stay at a budget hotel that offers a free buffet breakfast, you'll likely be satisfied when you get your own coffee in a paper cup. That's what you expected. But what if you stay at a five-star hotel, go to their restaurant for breakfast, and the server tells you the coffee is self-serve? That won't match up with your expectations of what the five-star experience should be, so it's likely you'll be dissatisfied.

So what are the drivers of perceived value? There is a set of three attributes that create the drivers: the people, the process, and the physical.

Figure 13-2, Perfect Satisfaction Drivers.

These three attributes work together. Any one alone is inadequate. The *people* need to be knowledgeable and friendly and instill trust with the customer, and the customer needs to perceive that they care. The *process* needs to be dependable and responsive to the customer's expectations, and it must deliver accurately. And the *physical* aspects—the environment, people, and equipment, as well as the communications and deliverables, and the feel, look, sound, taste, etc. of the product you provide—need to be in order. All three need to be in line with expectations to achieve satisfaction.

Your customer's expectations are shaped by external forces, which might include word of mouth from other customers, other outside sources of information that they have found through research or learning, and their past experiences with you or someone else. Their expectations are also influenced by your brand promise, as they perceive it.

SYSTEMS FOR CUSTOMER RETENTION

Since perceptions are determined by the satisfaction drivers against those expectations, you need to systemize the delivery of the drivers so that they match with or achieve what the customer expects. Now we will look at the systems you can implement to do that.

Customer feedback. The customer feedback systems are designed to collect information about how the customer experiences the delivery of your product or service. It begins with a survey.

You need to ask the key questions that will determine how the customer perceives and expects the satisfaction drivers you deliver. It's important to time the surveys correctly so you gauge their overall experience. Don't issue them immediately after every transaction but at a time when they can take into account their entire experience.

Then you need to set up key performance indicators that measure this, such as your responsiveness (as measured in the cycle time from the ask to the delivery), your accuracy and dependability (as measured by delivery in full, on time, in spec as described before), and your churn rate (the number of customers you are losing per any given period).

You must install audits or inspections of any of the physical drivers and the physical environment, or a quality assurance step in terms of the deliverables or products. In manufacturing, it's common to do a final inspection of the product before it is shipped. You need to do the same thing if you are in the service business or any other business where the customer interacts with any physical aspect. It might even be proofreading the emails that are sent for marketing.

Finally, you need to look at your sales trends. This year's sales versus last year's sales will tell the story as well, and that's the ultimate customer feedback system.

Satisfaction skill development. The purpose of the satisfaction skill development systems is to teach your team the people part of the drivers. It will require ongoing training, both in terms of new education and reinforcement of existing education. Usually, it's done on a quarterly basis to improve and maintain their service skills. You will need to work on their professional development, which would include the soft skills they need to interact with clients and customers and the routine updates of product knowledge they need so they can fulfill the expectation of knowledge about what you offer. You can use the principles and tools from Chapter 7, Performance Management, to manage the training and development process.

Customer connection. Your customer connection systems will enhance and improve your relationship with your key customers.

You begin with segmentation. Once again, follow the 80/20 principle here. First list and rank your customers by the amount of money they have spent with you in the last 12 months. Then analyze the numbers to find the 20% of the customers who provide 80% of the benefits. That 20% are the people who deserve and expect extra attention from you so they will keep coming back and spending with you.

The best way to provide the extra attention is to create a VIP or loyalty program that rewards them and gives them incentives to continue spending with you. The benefits of the program aren't necessarily discounts. Instead, they could be some added value such as tickets to events, VIP customer recognition awards, or dinners—anything over and above what your customers ordinarily would expect. When you implement the program, you need to set up key performance indicators to measure its effect and make sure it pays off, but more importantly, you want to study your VIPs because you want more of them. They happen to be your best source of referrals because they tend to refer like-kind prospects. So it's worth it to understand what exactly they are buying from you and stimulate referrals. You will want to promote the program to your customer base and encourage enrollment.

The next piece you need to put in place is your database and the way you communicate with your customers on an ongoing basis. With the software that is available now, it is fairly simple and easy to maintain contact with your customers and send them emails with very little effort. The purpose of the emails you send out isn't necessarily to promote your business but to provide value in some way by sharing some important information or a story or an item of interest that is truly valuable to them. An example of this would be a high-end remodeler who produces a quarterly newspaper that includes a checklist of home maintenance tips to accomplish. Although the remodeler doesn't generate major projects directly with the newsletter, they keep themselves top of mind with it so when people do choose to do a project, they are the first ones they think about. It's part of the reason that they have an 80% repeat business rate.

Finally, because not all customers are created equal, you will have to do some pruning. It's best to do the pruning periodically, usually once a year. To do it, you list your customers and score them on a scale from 1 to 10 where the score implies the following:

- 9–10: fans—customers who actively refer clients to you and advocate on your behalf
- 7–8: passive fans
- 4–6: customers on probation—customers who could be good if new expectations were set for them, and they were retrained and reeducated to pay on time or fit your business model.
- 1–3: wrong fits—customers who drag down and suck the energy out of your business because they bother your team, don't pay, or become vampires in one way or another.

The customers who scored 1, 2, and 3 are the ones you need to refer to one of your competitors so that they are no longer a part of the mix. As difficult as it is to get rid of customers, these ones are costing you too much in terms of aggravation, lost opportunity and time that you should instead be investing in your clients who scored 9 and 10 (or finding new ones).

Critical moments choreography. Finally, you need to choreograph the critical moments in your business. Those are the moments of truth that I mentioned earlier. Follow the 4-Step System Building Process outlined in Chapter 2 to design in detail what should happen each time a customer interacts with your team throughout their journey with you.

Then design an optimum experience. Script it and document it so that you have an ideal customer experience from beginning to end that you can model. Then train the team to follow this model.

CHAPTER 14

Conclusion

When I was a young man, I read a book written by Sam Walton called *Made in America*. It's the story of how he grew a five-and-ten store into Walmart, the largest retailer in America. It's a remarkable story. I thought about it a lot because I wanted to apply all the learnings to my own business. My conclusion was that their success was not one single thing; it was that they did a lot of things very well.

Therein lies the challenge for the business owner. It requires mastery of a wide array of skills and strategies and ideas to be successful. It's complex, it's moving quickly, and it's changing all the time. Hence the need for The Perfect Business Framework, which you can use to simplify your approach and accelerate your results as you take on the challenge of building your perfect business.

By now, you may have noticed both the good news and the bad news. The good news is that it costs very little in terms of cash to build the systems described in this book. The bad news is that it takes a lot of focused thought and diligent work. It is something that you can control, though, and it's worthwhile because it will bring you greater value, more time, and more cash flow if you stick with it.

I'd like to share with you a few observations based on my experience and the success of others to encourage you for those times when you will feel overwhelmed about the journey ahead.

First, it's not just about creating the systems; it's about bringing about change in the team, in the culture, and ultimately, in you as a leader. The best leaders are always learning and growing along with the business. It's not an option. Your business will grow only as fast as you learn, and it will grow only to the limits of your capability.

Second, learn to love it. Learn to love rolling up your sleeves and solving the problems, as difficult as they might seem. When you start to see the results, it will become quite a lot of fun.

Third, it's important to persist. You won't hit any home runs, but you should hit lots of singles, and over time, they will add up. It also pays to have patience because there will be times when it won't come quickly enough for you.

Fourth, letting go is going to be difficult, but do it anyway. You didn't give up teaching your child how to ride a bicycle because you were afraid they might crash. Developing your team is no different.

Finally, get some help both from inside your team and from the outside. There is no such thing as a self-made man. Anyone who has accomplished anything significant has had a lot of help along the way.

Now, get started.

If you need help, you can find me at www.johnsheridan.com.

About the Author

John Sheridan is an advisor to small business owners throughout the United States known for his work on systemization as the key to business transformation. He brings over 30 years of practical business experience to his work, with operating and investing experience in businesses large and small.

His Perfect Business Framework was born of his experience both running and advising business owners in developing and implementing systems that transform entrepreneurial companies into professionally managed and systematized enterprises that produce predictable results.

John is a graduate of The Boston College School of Management with a concentration in finance and began his career in industrial real estate marketing and sales. His work led to a career in construction and real estate development leading and managing profitable, growing businesses ranging in size from startups to public company business units.

Since 2006, John has helped successful business owners to grow profits, build great teams, and create lasting value in a variety of industries including professional services, software and technology, manufacturing, construction, and distribution.

Building great people who build great companies is what gives purpose to his work. John resides in Lawrenceville, New Jersey, and he is a Past President of The Rotary Club of Trenton, New Jersey.

Printed in Great Britain
by Amazon